The Perfect Alibi:

Freedom from the Drive for Personal Perfection

Eric K. Sweitzer, Ph.D.

2006

ISBN 1-4116-7312-3

Printed in the United States of America

To my wife, Susan,
and my three daughters,
Katherine, Meredith, and Jenna

Who, as gifts to me from God,
have enabled me to experience
the meaning of His grace

Contents

INTRODUCTION

A Tale of Two Travelers

Alice was born the oldest of five children in a basically stable, church-going family. Her father was a decent man who provided adequately for the family; but to do so, often worked two and even three jobs at least 6 days per week. This meant that the mother had a lot on her own plate caring for her large family; and Alice, being the firstborn, was given significant responsibilities at an early age.

Mother and Father would remark that she would have to act as "Mom's little helper." She had an important place in her world, and was rewarded with praise when she made sure that household tasks were completed and that younger siblings were dressed, fed, sent to bed, etc. As Alice began school, she found that working hard also brought good grades and praise from teachers and parents. Mom and Dad would tell Alice that they never had to worry about her – she could always be depended upon at home and school.

Alice continued to play this responsible role throughout adolescence and young adulthood. Church was yet another arena in which hard work and conscientiousness seemed to pay off. Attending services regularly, memorizing scripture, daily Bible reading and prayer were all disciplines that just came naturally to someone like Alice, who learned to view herself as a young person who always did the "right thing." Even as a teenager, while younger siblings and peers were beginning to argue with parents over schoolwork, dating, church attendance, choice of music and movies, Alice quietly continued on the pathway of compliance with the rules for life that the adult community had laid out clearly for her.

The sense of personal accomplishment and self-worth that Alice derived from being so responsible outweighed any criticism or even ostracism that occasionally came from peers. She figured that if people did not like her, it was only because they were jealous of her many accomplishments and accolades that began to pile up in the form of academic rewards and Sunday School perfect attendance pins.

Given her stellar performance, Alice was readily accepted into the Christian college of her choice, where she continued her journey towards success. When professors handed out assignments at the beginning of a new semester, Alice was the type of student who would head right from class to the library, in order to map out her plan of attack. Alice would choose paper topics and devise a study schedule for the entire 12-week semester, so that she would be sure to complete all work in a timely and efficient fashion. No last minute "all-nighters" for me, she would think to herself: "I will do everything I can do to be sure that I achieve my goal of academic excellence."

Since college is not just about studying, Alice's roommate attempted to interest her in various extra-curricular programs and ministries. She agreed to join one or two, but did so reluctantly, because it was the "right thing" to do, even though she feared the extra time involvement would jeopardize her academic goals. Alice managed fairly well during those four years, even allowing enough time to date and meet her mate for life, Murray. At the end of each semester, Alice would feel a great sense of relief that her hard work had allowed her to maintain a high grade point average. She could relax for only a few days however, before she would start planning for the next semester and wondering about her courses, whether she could handle the course load for yet another 12 weeks. In fact, the more she succeeded, the more Alice assumed that others expected her to maintain such a high level of performance. Thus, each new challenge became slightly more stressful because Alice believed she had to do at least as well, if not even better, than previously.

By the way, Alice marveled at other students who just didn't seem to "sweat" things as much as she did. How could her friend, Karen, actually forget to hand in a paper, and still go out and enjoy herself at a movie that same evening? How could Murray get a C in Chemistry and not be devastated? How could kids on the ski team take off for the weekend and not bring their books with them? Towards her closest friends, including Murray, Alice even felt a sense of responsibility – they obviously needed her help to perform as well as she did. Some of her attempts to come to their aid were well received; others were politely refused, causing Alice to feel somewhat hurt and confused.

Alice achieved her bachelor's degree with high honors, and married Murray a month after graduation. Her next challenge was teaching 5th grade, while Murray went on to law school. Moving into their first apartment and finding their first church, Alice had much to do in order to get ready for the next "semester" of life. Between preparing for teaching, household responsibilities, and now activities at church, Alice found it difficult to get everything done in her usual "timely and efficient" manner. She began to develop occasional headaches and sometimes had difficulty falling asleep after a busy day.

Murray seemed to chug along through their new life together in a more relaxed fashion. He never seemed to worry about paying bills, getting chores done, planning for the future, etc., so Alice assumed that somebody had better worry, or nothing would get done. It would have to be one of her roles in the marriage.

Alice also had some concerns about relating to her in-laws. She never was quite sure where she stood with them, and this fueled her drive to be the best wife that she could be to their son, assuming this would put her in good standing with them.

Life progressed in this same fashion for a few more years until Murray finished law school, and he and Alice decided it was time to start a family. Little Sarah was born three years into the marriage, and Thomas followed 2 years later.

Alice now accepted the challenge of maintaining her commitments to the church, keeping up with household tasks, continuing to be a loving sensitive wife, daughter-in-law, and now an attentive mother of two active children. Generally, things seemed to go according to plan, yet Alice slowly but surely began to feel overwhelmed by all her duties. Headaches became more frequent and more increasingly intense.

One particular evening, Alice went to bed with a lot on her mind. Her in-laws were coming for Sarah's 4th birthday the next afternoon, and Alice had so much to do to get ready. The house needed cleaning;

laundry had piled up; gifts needed to be wrapped; and a cake made. Murray seemed to be pressuring her, albeit nicely, to make sure everything was in order for the party. Alice attempted to sleep, knowing that she would need to be rested for the arduous day ahead, but her mind just continued to race.

The next morning, she woke after only a few hours of fitful sleep with a massive headache and intense nausea. She couldn't go on with her day and had to call her family physician for an appointment. After listening patiently and running a few medical tests, her doctor diagnosed her with "burnout" and suggested she try to slow down her hectic lifestyle, and that she meet with a counselor. Reluctantly, Alice agreed to accept the referral and thus began a new chapter in her life's journey as she began to explore the root causes of her stress.

Our second life-traveler is a young man named Ben. Unlike Alice, Ben generally avoided responsibility rather than unquestionably accepting new demands and challenges. Ben was the youngest of three brothers in a high-achieving family. His father was a well-respected radiologist, who valued the pursuit of excellence in every major area of life – academics, sports, and music. Dad was a "Renaissance Man" who could do everything well. Ben's two brothers, Tyler and Conner, were following in their father's footsteps. Tyler had been salutorian of his high school class, captain of the football team, and after graduation from a pre-med program at an Ivy League college, was sailing through medical school. Conner, two years behind Tyler, was also an honors student in college, a first-rate hockey player, and even found time to win awards in trumpet competitions. Like his brother, college scholarships were easily procured, and Conner was enjoying his undergraduate years as a pre-law student.

Along came Ben, an 11th grader, whose academic record was rather spotty compared to those of his older brothers. Ben had done quite well himself in elementary school, being told that he also had very high potential based on early standardized testing. Without too much effort, Ben was able to pull A's and B's in grade school, but as junior high began, his performance became more erratic. A 65 could follow a 100 on a test in English; a B in Social Studies then a C next semester. When asked by his parents and teachers why such inconsistency, Ben could only shrug his shoulders.

Athletically, Ben also showed promise as a little leaguer, but never seemed to try his best. Again, coaches and parents raved about his potential, but consistency on the playing field seemed to elude him. Dad and older brothers almost had to bribe Ben to try out for the junior high team. By the spring of his freshman year, Ben's grades were becoming questionable enough that he chose not to try out for the high school team. His parents were disappointed, but agreed that grades must come before sports. A strange pattern began to develop as Ben's high school career progressed. He seemed to set himself up deliberately for failure. When he had plenty of time to prepare for a test, he would wait until the last minute and try to cram.

Procrastination became his rule for written assignments as well. During these high school years, Ben hung out with some friends who had started a band, and he discovered that he was a natural drummer. This became his true passion, and Ben spent hours in the family basement practicing on the drum set that he had purchased with summer earnings. The night before a big chemistry test, Ben admittedly ignored the books and played his drums well into the wee hours of the morning. He was not prepared mentally or physically for the exam; and hence earned his first failing grade. Ben's parents were increasingly frustrated, never experiencing such a challenge with their first two sons. At first, they tried to understand and encourage; and then, as time progressed, frustration led to attempts to discipline and pressure Ben into "living up to his academic potential." The more the pressure, the more Ben would passively resist. By the spring of his junior year, he was failing three major subjects, and the school guidance counselor warned that he might need to repeat his junior year. When most of his friends were beginning to consider colleges, Ben faced the prospect of summer school. The "last straw" for Ben's parents was when Ben came home from band practice acting somewhat strange and exuding an odor that they knew was not Old Spice cologne. Ben barked out, "Yeah, I've been smoking pot for a while now…What are you going to do about it!" At this point, his parents sought their pastor's assistance in locating a counselor who might help with this desperate situation.

Alice and Ben represent two travelers on the pathway of life. Each faces a fundamental challenge that every human being encounters: How do we negotiate the demands and responsibilities inherent in daily life? Alice tended to keep trying harder, no matter how complex her life became, until she virtually crashed. Young Ben, on the other hand, sensed that he could not maintain the pace that he thought was expected of him, so he slowly fell out of the race altogether; and instead, invested time and energy in an activity that provided an immediate sense of competence and success.

The chapters which follow, chart the process through which each of us negotiates life. We are born into a world of standards and expectations to which we must respond as a young child. As time progresses, we create our own internalized set of self-expectations, which determines the way we relate to life events, towards other people, and even towards God Himself. At some point in our experience, we develop one of the two styles represented by our two travelers – we either try too hard, or we give up on life – and often we combine the two approaches as we continue on a perpetually stressful and frustrating life's journey ("Most men live quiet lives of desperation").

My hope is that the chapters which follow will not only help explain how these dynamics develop and wreak havoc in our lives; but more importantly, will direct us towards an alternative way of handling life's demands. An alternative that allows us to set goals and objectives, and strive for excellence, especially as professing Christians, without over-exerting ourselves or avoiding life's challenges entirely.

PART ONE:

THE PROCESS OF ENSLAVEMENT

Chapter One:

Enslavement by Others: *The Birth of Shame*

We are born into this world as helpless, vulnerable infants who have no other option than to trust in the environment around us for physical and emotional nurturance. Our immediate environment is, of course, our family. No family is perfect. Some families are more loving and caring than others, and there are some that definitely do merit the currently popular label, "dysfunctional." The degrees of health or maturity of any family lies along a continuum, running from "very dysfunctional" at one end, to "healthier" at the other end; but no family can legitimately claim perfection.

One primary criterion for determining where a family falls on this continuum is the degree to which children feel a natural sense of love and acceptance, as opposed to such approval having to be earned by meeting certain standards. In theological terms, the question could be phrased: "To what extent does grace become the basis for approval?" Or conversely, "To what degree must a child 'earn salvation' by following certain prescribed rules or standards?" Of course, I am not equating family acceptance with one's righteous status before God. Yet it is on the level of human relationships that we begin to grasp God's acceptance of us, and it is on that same level that we carry out our lives in response to God's acceptance.

Rules To Live By:

Every family has its own "***Rules of Approval.***" They determine what a child must do or not do, say or not say, or even be or not be, in order to feel approval by the family. This need to be acceptable, to "belong," to "fit in," or simply to be loved, is undoubtedly a child's greatest driving force, even from the earliest stages of infancy. An infant quickly senses, well before he or she can think or speak in verbal terms, that certain rules must be fulfilled in order to receive nurturing approval.

Such "rules of approval" can take many different forms. Some are directly spoken; others are subtly implied. Some are very clearly stated; others are confusing and vague. Some never change; others are erratic and inconsistent. Some are virtually impossible to fulfill; others require little effort.

In the context of counseling, clients are asked to describe their family environment and then try to identify what would have been some of the particular "rules of approval." I usually ask, "Given what you have just described, what would you as a young boy/girl have to have done or not done, said or not said, in order to feel approved?" One female client quickly responded to my question by saying, "Well, to begin with, you had to be a boy!" Another man told me that no matter what one said or did, it had to correspond with his father's philosophy of life. In other words, the major rule of that family was simply, "Father is always right; even when he is wrong, he is right."

We also must keep in mind that the family unit is itself influenced by other rules of approval from the larger social environment. Socio-economic levels (poverty vs. wealth) create certain rules regarding how much money, material possessions or education a person or family must have in order to fit in. Our American culture has many "rules" that influence us and our families, aided by the powerful force of the media. Women must be beautiful, slender, intelligent, and wealthy professionals, and be wonderful wives and mothers, also. Men must be handsome, physically strong, athletic, financially successful, a "jack of all trades", and stoically impervious to hurt and pain. Race can also be a factor. One must be white, black, Hispanic, Oriental, etc., in order to fit in at school or the neighborhood.

In this context, peer influences are especially strong. A woman reported feeling a sense of shame as she went to school each day, attempting to hide the bottoms of her shoes, which would have revealed sheets of cardboard to cover over the holes. Likewise, a few years ago our American culture was pressuring school-aged children to wear a certain type of jacket with the logos of certain professional sports teams. If they could not afford the exorbitant price for such an item, they would not receive full approval from peers. Parents, many of whom really could not afford such a purchase, would buy such items anyway, in order to follow their own rule of approval: "A good parent always provides their children with whatever is in style."

Those of us who attend churches regularly are influenced by sets of rules. There are forms of Evangelical Protestant "culture", charismatic or Pentecostal "subcultures" or Roman Catholic "subcultures", which explicitly and/or implicitly suggest how we should live our lives in order to be accepted. Yet, I would argue that any "subculture" outside of the realm of Christianity, has its own rules of approval as well. Even if you were raised by parents who were members of the "Hell's Angels", you would quickly learn a set of rules, expectations, or standards unique to that group. You would have to wear the "right" kind of clothing, ride a certain type of motorcycle, and engage in certain behaviors defined by the group as acceptable.

Our sense of personal value and worth is determined by how well we, as children, perceive ourselves to have successfully followed the "rules." Simply put, the more we believe that we played by the rules and received approval, the more positively we begin to think and feel about ourselves. Conversely, the more we perceive ourselves to have failed to follow the rules and thus received disapproval, the more negatively we have learned to view ourselves. The degree to which we seem to be following the rules affects three key areas:

1. The manner in which I think and feel about myself.
2. The way I think, feel about, and relate to other people; and, how I perceive them to think, feel about and relate towards, me.
3. The way in which I think, feel about and relate to God; and, how I perceive Him to think, feel about and relate to me.

Before examining these three areas in further detail, one crucial factor connected to this notion of "rules of approval" must be clarified. Our response to the rules is strongly affected by the way in which children view reality. Their view is narrow, limited and self-focused. I like to explain the situation this way: A child views himself as the center of the universe. He or she is the most important and most powerful person in that universe. At age 8, one of my daughters was explaining to me how when she "was little" she used to think everybody, including her mother and me, were in a play that revolved around her as the main character. Her entire philosophy of life was summed up by the perception that others existed only to play a role in her own life.

When something bad or painful occurs in the child's universe (or "play"), the child reasons in the following manner:

> a.) *Something bad has happened in my universe.*
> b.) *Something must have caused it to happen.*
> c.) *I am the most powerful force in my universe.*
> d.) *I must have caused this bad thing to happen.*
> e.) *Therefore, I must be bad myself; there must be something wrong with me; I must have failed to follow the rules.*

Children do not have a more complete and well-informed perspective on life and thus do not understand the inappropriate nature of the various rules they are exposed to. They do not grasp the reality, totally unrelated to their own personal value or worth, that the adults in their lives are limited, imperfect and also sinful creatures. An adult looking back upon her own childhood can sincerely state that it was not her fault, that as a child, her father sexually abused her. Yet, when the abuse actually occurred at say, seven years of age, that little girl would not have reasoned as an adult. Instead, she would have assumed that, because something bad happened within her universe, she must have done something to cause or deserve it. Such logic becomes entrenched in the subconscious mind and remains there as the years go on.

A female client once experienced a prolonged period of severe "flashback" memories of violent sexual abuse during her childhood. When she returned to an awareness of herself now, as an adult, the very first words I heard her utter were these: "What must I have done to deserve this abuse?" You see, she was assuming that she must have failed to observe certain rules of approval in her own family, and the abuse was her deserved punishment.

I cannot tell this particular case vignette without also being reminded of a scene from the classic movie, *The Sound of Music.* A romantic scene occurs when Maria and the Captain finally declare their love for one another, while retreating from a sudden rainstorm in a beautiful gazebo. Maria declares her surprise and joy through a song, which includes the line: "*Somewhere in my youth or childhood, I must have done something good...*" While I have enjoyed watching that scene and the entire movie with my family, that one line has always disturbed me. The implied "truth" here is that doing the right things necessarily results in positive rewards. Sometimes in our lives, this is true, of course. However, this line of reasoning leaves open the reverse situation as well – "*If I do not follow the rules properly, I deserve to be punished.*"

If Maria had continued to struggle as a frustrated novitiate in her religious order, and she never found the degree of fulfillment that the movie depicts, than she could have assumed that she messed up somewhere along the way. She would have failed to follow the rules, at least in her own mind, and then what would that say about her value as a person?

What children are not able to do is evaluate the appropriateness of rules; nor can they judge the health or maturity of adults, institutions or entire cultures that have developed the rules. They assume that the rules are written in stone and must be followed. If this cannot be done, the fault must lie in the child alone, not in the realm of the adult world that developed the rules. Children assume that they have violated rules when forms of sexual, physical, or emotional abuse have occurred in their lives. The latter category can include many forms of indirect abuse. Examples would be a manipulative parent blaming a young child for their own emotional outbursts: "If you didn't whine so much, I wouldn't have broken the coffee table. Now we can't afford to have a birthday party for your brother because we have to buy new table!"

Children assume they are responsible for all kinds of problems that adults have created - marital conflict, divorce, and alcohol problems - and also for problems that are really no one's fault. A five-year-old boy whose father dies suddenly in a car accident will use logic like this to interpret what has happened:

My father is no longer here. He no longer pays attention to ME.

Since I am so important, I must have done something for Dad not to be here for ME anymore. Therefore, I must be bad.

This may actually sound preposterous to our adult ears. That is because we fail to appreciate how differently children perceive the world and their place in it.

Developmental psychologists remind us that children are "egocentric." This is not necessarily synonymous with self-centeredness, which is an outgrowth of our inborn sinful nature. Egocentrism simply refers to an early stage of cognitive growth in which, due to limited life experience, a young child perceives the outside world to revolve around her needs, desires, ideas, and behaviors. The child is the main character in her play, and all the action, positive or negative, which occurs on her life stage, revolves around the quality of her performance in the leading role.

Even in a home with well-meaning, well-educated Christian parents, children's logic can lead to negative self-blame. I use myself as an example of a parent who unintentionally created a situation that could have been grossly misinterpreted by my daughters. At the time, my two older girls were about ages four and six. One evening at the dinner table, I criticized them for not eating properly with their fork, knife and spoon. My tone of voice was probably derogatory, which did not help matters. Fortunately, I caught myself quickly, realizing that I had never taken the time to instruct them as to the proper use of eating utensils (perhaps my wife had, but I knew I had not!).

I certainly cannot know for sure, but each of my daughters' internal responses may have gone this way:

> *Daddy is telling ME that I am doing something wrong.*
> *He has never taught ME how to use these things, but*
> *Daddies always know what is right. He must not have*
> *taught ME because I should naturally know how to do*
> *this MYSELF. Apparently, I don't know how, so there*
> *must be something inherently wrong with ME.*

A young child, of course, does not verbalize his or her thoughts and feelings in this manner. A five-year-old girl does not write such interpretations down in her daily diary. However, these negative messages are being developed in the subconscious mind, even in a very young child, who cannot yet speak or write. It is precisely because such messages are "encoded" at an early age, beyond the realm of conscious awareness, that we carry them right into adulthood. The "rules of approval" are likewise transferred into adulthood, albeit for the most part, unconsciously.

A woman told me that in her alcoholic childhood home, one clearly stated rule was, "If you don't have anything important to say, don't say anything at all." As a child, she interpreted this to create the negative self-message of, "I have nothing important to say," and therefore, "I must be unimportant." She was in my office, partly because as a woman now in her thirties, she had continued to live by this rule, which led to negative consequences in her approach to relationships and current life situations.

While it may be crude in some respects, I use the analogy of a personal computer to describe how these internalized rules operate within us. Encoded on the hard drive of my personal computer are numerous coded messages that run the entire system. Being basically illiterate when it comes to understanding computer languages and the principles of programming, I really have no idea what is programmed on to that drive. However, when I boot up the system, I observe that my computer can do no more or no less than what the messages on its drive allow it to do.

It seems to me that the hard drive is like our subconscious mind. Messages, of which we are primarily unaware, have been encoded on our thinking process since childhood. The younger we were when these messages were received, the more we may have personalized them in a negative fashion (*"It's my fault – there's something wrong with me"*); and the more deeply embedded those messages have become because we are unaware of them and our interpretations of them. It is our lack of awareness that gives them power over ue.

I tell my clients that, like all of us, they are now adults with adult bodies, intellects, skills, areas of knowledge and experience.

However, they are continuing to function in accordance with certain primary "childlike" messages, associated with key rules of approval, which are still having a profoundly negative effect upon their lives.

To stick with the computer analogy, our first task is to take out the old program that has been running our life's system for so long, and begin to expose and identify the negative commands and messages. Our second task is to choose whether we want to continue operating our life's system based on these particular messages, or whether we want to re-program the system with healthier, more Biblically based messages. In its simplest form, I have just described the therapeutic process. Yet, this process of psychological and spiritual growth need not be confined to the offices of a "professional" setting. These same principles can be applied to anyone who is seeking to know God more deeply, by first evaluating himself or herself more clearly.

Roles and Rules

Related to the notion of "rules of approval" is the fact that children assume various roles in their "families of origin." To understand this concept of "roles", we must begin with the premise that a family, like any social group, is a type of system. Every system is comprised of a set of individual parts, each of which has its own function. As in the New Testament concept of the body of Christ, these individual members or parts make their unique, individual contributions to the overall functioning of the entire system. These parts inter-relate in a manner that enables the system to work towards a particular set of goals and objectives. A similar analogy would be an athletic team, on which individual players, assuming specific positions or roles, all contribute to the eventual goal of winning.

In a nuclear family, the ultimate goal is the cohesiveness of the system. Children assume various roles, especially when adults fail to play their parenting roles properly, in order to help maintain an environment in which, at least, their physical needs are cared for, and if possible, their emotional needs as well. Some roles are more natural than others, such as those determined by birth order. Much research has been done on what appears to be general truths about older children, middle children, youngest children, etc. An eldest child, for example, may play a leadership role towards younger siblings, and a younger child may assume the role of follower. Children have a need to not only maintain the family system, but also to belong or "fit in.", i.e., they strive for a sense of unique identity. Therefore, a younger sibling, whose older brother may be the one who excels in academics, may seek out another non-academic realm in which to gain notoriety in the family.

Here is where the "rules" idea comes in again. The younger sibling may perceive that a family rule is, "You must succeed academically in order to be accepted." Due to a sense of competition, the younger may assume that she could never achieve to the same degree as the older. Her next option would be to "find her niche" in some other realm, such as music or sports, or through socializing with peers. Equally possible, however, would be the option of actually trying to supersede the successes of the elder sibling. In other words, if a child perceives a certain rule to be in operation, he or she can either attempt to play by that rule, or to find some other arena in which to gain approval from, and identity within, the family system. The degree to which the child is successful in pursuing either direction determines how positively or negatively the child feels about him or herself.

I am reminded of this dynamic whenever I play a game with a child in the counseling context. A child with a fairly damaged sense of self will attempt to beat me in a simple game such as "Uno". Being primarily a game of luck more than skill, the child and I are evenly matched (I've been beaten many times by preschoolers!). Yet, the insecure child appears to live by some rule of approval such as, "I must win, because winners are good and losers are bad." Some children, if they have lost a few consecutive games, will demand that we play more, even if the session is ending, with hopes that they can finally "prove themselves" through victory. Others take the opposite tack: They attempt to change the rules in the midst of a game to their advantage, or may desire to terminate the game and choose some other activity, usually one they know they can win.

One young man, whose parents had recently been involved in a very hostile divorce, described to me the sense of being stretched by each parent in either direction. Therefore, he could never win! Each of his parent's desires and interests always seemed to take preference over his well-being and desires. In a sense, he had given up on attempting to gain true approval from either mother or father. His life was out of his control, as is true of any child in an abusive situation. This boy responded by developing his own life rule: "Control others before they control you."

This approach to situations and relationships was evident in virtually every counseling session. He would manipulate as best he could so that he chose the game or activity, and he determined the rules. Half way through a game of checkers, if he perceived himself to be losing, he would invent new moves, since the standard rules no longer served his purpose. On one occasion, he brought in a deck of playing cards and launched into a lengthy explanation of the rules for a new game he had devised. After listening for a while, I made the observation that there was actually no way for either player to win, to which he responded, "That's the whole point!" The game, as he devised it, became an apt metaphor for how he perceived his life situation: he couldn't win.

Both rules and roles become intensified in families that are more "dysfunctional". Titles have been given to the various roles that children can play, such as the *"Hero"*, the *"Scapegoat"*, the *"Parentified Child"*, or the *"Family Mascot"*. Each role has at least two purposes: First, any role, be it positive in society's eyes (e.g., the *Hero* who succeeds academically), or negative (the *Scapegoat* who always gets into trouble), or more neutral (the *"Lost child"* who is the very quiet, overly compliant child), *takes the focus of attention in the family away from problems at the parental level.*

Secondly, *any role*, even a negative or neutral one, *allows the child to have some sense of identity, purpose, and thus importance within the family system.* As teachers have long observed about children with behavioral problems, such kids seem to figure that "negative attention is at least better than no attention at all." Even the more neutral roles are designed to deter further attention being given to the parental distress, and will allow the child to feel they are helping in some way.

For example, a child may "melt into the woodwork" as much as possible, so that by their inconspicuousness they can avoid arousing rage in an alcoholic father.

The result is that by playing individual roles, or combinations of roles, as is often the case, children's "rules of approval" become more specific. The children playing negative roles assume, "*I must act-out to get attention, and at least some type of approval.*" Within the positive roles, the rules are, "*I must be well behaved and I must perform flawlessly in order to keep the family going and be accepted myself.*" The neutral roles involve rules such as, "Just do your own thing quietly. Don't draw attention to yourself by either being too bad or too good. This is the only way to really survive life."

Much has been written on the characteristics and dynamics of what social scientists now call "dysfunctional" families, and our attempt here is not to duplicate that material. For our current purposes, it is helpful to define a "dysfunctional" family as one in which children sense a strong need to earn their approval, rather than a natural sense of being valued for who they are as a person.

The dysfunction always begins at the parental level, due to emotional, relational, and spiritual immaturity within both parents. Such immaturity is expressed through marital conflict, emotional volatility, and a variety of addictions. The latter include chemical addictions (alcohol and other drugs), behavioral addictions (e.g. gambling, sexual addictions, eating disorders), but also more "socially accepted" addictions such as workaholism, or even over-involvement in religious activities.

In the midst of such parental dysfunction, rules of approval become extreme rather than more balanced. Parents' problems are, in themselves, the outgrowth of adults, who in their own mind have never successfully fulfilled the rules of approval of their own childhood. *Adulthood becomes an arena in which parents attempt to achieve, finally, what they think they failed to do as children - be acceptable.* Sensing this failure, although primarily on an unconscious level, the parents now attempt to finally succeed by the rules, or take the opposite approach of rebelling against them. Yet, even in the latter case, the parents internally blame themselves for not ever totally fulfilling the "real rules." As a result of all this struggling, the parent is unable to establish reasonable rules and consistently communicate them to their own children. Thus, extremes result, which can run in either direction --too many rules or no rules at all; rules that are communicated very clearly, but are extreme, and those that are not communicated well at all; those that are consistently unreasonable, and those that are unpredictable.

One more striking example emphasizes the fact that roles and rules can be established at very early, even "preverbal" stages. I once counseled a young couple who were trapped in an abusive vicious cycle. The husband would physically beat the wife, especially when he would find her drinking. The more she drank, the more he would beat her; the more he beat her, the more she would drink, etc.

As I was discussing this with the couple, their children were occupying themselves in my waiting room. The youngest was a girl, not yet two years old. During the course of our session, this child interrupted several times by knocking on the door, coming in, and asking for a toy or crayons. As time progressed, she continued to come in about every five minutes, even though she eventually ran out of things to ask for.

As this was getting very disruptive, I suggested that perhaps this little girl was attempting to tell us something through her behavior. Before I could even offer a theory, the parents quickly declared, "Oh, she does this all the time at home, especially when we're fighting." I did not need to state the obvious: A young girl, less than 2 years old, had already at her age, assumed the role of keeping peace in the household, by attempting to draw attention to herself whenever parental conflict would begin. Now, this young lady, when she becomes an adult, will most likely not recall this and many similar incidents from her early childhood. However, the assumptions about herself and about other people, which began before age two, encoded unconsciously upon her mind, will still be affecting her in adulthood if she is not given the opportunity to become aware of them.

To summarize, children interpret the world around them, beginning with the family system, by creating "rules of approval". Their environment, particularly parental figures, can directly and powerfully dictate such rules to children either by their interaction with them (forms of abuse), or lack of personal involvement with them (forms of neglect). In the latter case, children are left to assume that they failed to follow certain rules. In either case, whether rules are explicitly stated or not, children devise their own inner rules based on their interpretation of what is happening in their world.

Children then respond to the rules by either attempting to fulfill them, or rebelling against them. In the first instance, children's frantic strivings are ultimately fruitless because the dysfunctional rules are virtually impossible to fulfill. The result is the underlying worry that "I will never be good enough." Yet if children attempt to rebel against the rules, they are never actually set free from them either. The child who assumes he must get all A's in order to be approved, may deliberately flunk out. He then becomes enslaved to his own rebellion, unable to determine what level of academic performance he himself is truly capable of achieving. Down deep, he can only agree that, ideally, he should be achieving the same standards that he attempts to change or run from. Otherwise, he would not work so hard to disassociate himself from those rules or standards.

Rules are developed primarily at unconscious levels of awareness, and are then carried with the child through each stage of life into adulthood. As adults, we have matured physically and intellectually, yet our emotional, relational and spiritual growth is thwarted by the same unconscious rules of approval that hinder our experience of God's grace. All such rules, and the family roles from which they are derived, are based on performance rather than grace. Our sense of self becomes based on the degree to which we perceive ourselves to have followed the rules.

To help you, the reader, begin to identify some of your own significant "Rules of Approval", let's use the following diagram:

THINGS HAPPEN (events, situations, relationships)

WE INTERPRET WHAT THEY MEAN TO US

WE EXPERIENCE FEELINGS IN RESPONSE
TO OUR INTERPRETATIONS

WE DEVELOP BEHAVIORS IN
RESPONSE TO OUR FEELINGS

This progression is relatively simple, but is quite profound in that it underlies how we understand and react to the world around us. The basic principle behind this little model is this: Events in themselves are not significant; it is how we interpret them that is crucial. In other words, the meaning we attribute to events, situations, and relationships is more powerful than they are themselves.

As we have already explained, children attribute meaning through the lens of "ego-centrism", with themselves as the center of their own universe. Thus, when significant things happen, especially negative things, the child's limited and somewhat distorted perceptions create inaccurate, but very powerful meanings. As also stated earlier, because such "meaning making" occurs unconsciously, these powerful interpretations are carried throughout life, right into adulthood. Interpretations are made in relation to one's self, other people, and ultimately God Himself. In keeping with the progression diagrammed above, interpretations lead to feelings, which in turn lead to behaviors.

Take the example of a person, who as a young child, was severely emotionally abused, perhaps by family members as well as peers. Being ridiculed, criticized, and manipulated, the child would form the reasonable assumption that there must be something wrong with him to merit such continual disapproval. As far as other people, they obviously cannot be trusted. Even his own family members, who say they love him, are eventually going to betray him. If such perceptions are strong enough, they could create a sense of paranoia towards the outside world.

If he thinks this way, then obviously he would feel generally fearful and distrusting towards others. If the feelings are intense enough, "paranoid" behavior will result - avoiding, hiding, and attempting to protect himself.

Let's picture an unfortunate person, we'll call him Frank, now as an adult, at a church function. After the morning service is a coffee hour, to which he comes with much fear and trepidation. He is assuming people will not want to talk with him; because just like when he was a child, they will eventually find out there is something unacceptable about him. Frank's feelings of anxiety express themselves in such behaviors as standing alone in a corner and avoiding eye contact with others.

Perhaps two or three other men, engaged in conversation, notice Frank standing off by himself. As fairly mature Christians, they feel concerned for Frank, sensing that he is uncomfortable, and begin to discuss quietly amongst themselves how they might approach him. Meanwhile, Frank happens to look up just as one of the group is glancing at him and while they are talking about him. Guess what Frank concludes? You're right – "See, those guys *are* talking about me...They are probably making fun of me."

What has just occurred is the start of a vicious cycle. Frank's original experiences as a child were interpreted by him, as having a negative meaning for himself and for others' intentions towards him. This provides an "interpretive context" or "grid" for future event, situations, and relationships. Therefore, now as an adult, Frank's interpretations lead to feelings of anxiety, resulting in avoidant behavior, which is observed by others.

Frank's behavior does not cause others to react in a certain way. It simply provides a situation to which others react, given their own "interpretive filters". Their responses to a person hiding in a corner, looking down at his feet, are predictable and natural. Yet, Frank observes their responses, and interprets them in a manner that only reinforces his original negative thinking about himself and others, and only increases his anxiety, creating more avoidant behavior, and the cycle repeats itself incessantly.

At whatever point in his life Frank learns about God, even solid Biblical teaching is translated through the filter of his interpretive system. Remember, of course, that such "filtering" is primarily unconscious, and thus remains powerful. Frank could achieve a Ph.D. in Biblical studies or theology - he could know all the right ideas about God on a conscious level. HOWEVER, it is the unconscious interpretive filter that really drives the way Frank relates to God as a Person. Can you see how Frank's filter affects his relationship with the One whom he theoretically knows to be a loving, caring, gracious Father?

Now, the point I am trying to make, of course, is that we all are Franks to one degree or another. We all have sensed since childhood that there is something wrong with us because we have not lived up to certain standards, or followed specific "rules of approval." We assume that others are, or will be, aware of our inadequacy, and will eventually withdraw from, if not reject us, entirely. Our resultant feelings of anxiety and depression lead us to withdraw from others in certain ways (we will examine them in detail later), and then we are left wondering why people don't want to accept us. We conclude, of course, that we are not worthy of their acceptance. This "closed loop" of thinking will go on uninterrupted, all through our lives, affecting us to one extent or another, unless it is recognized and arrested.

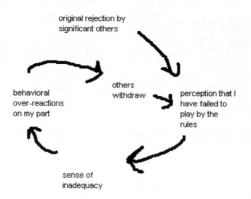

Identifying My Own Rules of Approval

Take this opportunity to begin investigate the "rules" that have probably driven your life even up to the present time. The progression outlined above, resulting in a "closed loop", or vicious cycle, can help us discover the key rules that we play by. Beginning at any point in the cycle, look for clues in your current responses to events, situations, and relationships:

1. Perhaps you can easily identify significant "things" that have happened to you, beginning in early childhood. If so, then ask yourself the question, "What would a young child have thought in response to such a situation about him/herself and other people?" Given that situation, how would a child have attempted to gain approval from others? What would he or she have to do, not do, be or not be, say or not say, to be accepted by family members, peer group, or other social groups? In other words, what would have been the *rules of approval* that ideally would have needed to be met?
2. How successful did the child think he or she was in fulfilling the rules? What ideas or assumptions were then made about himself, others, and ultimately God?
3. What feelings would have naturally emerged within the child in response to one's self and others?
4. What kinds of behaviors would have resulted from such feelings?
5. What kinds of predictable reactions would occur in other people in response to my behaviors?
6. How would I tend to interpret these reactions of others towards me?

If your memory of childhood situations is vague, then look at your current functioning in life. What rules you play by now as an adult are reflected in how you often feel, how you behaviorally react to events, people, and situations, and how people often respond to you. Look for recurring themes or trends in any of these areas.

By the way, dreams can involve such intense themes, and as such, give us clues to what rules we are attempting to play by. For example, the common dream theme of always trying to get to a destination, but never quite getting there, would tell us that probably both historically and currently, we perceive ourselves to be failing to fulfill certain rules.

While we may not be consciously aware of it, we may experience tremendous frustration in our attempts to win the approval of certain people in our waking life. This current struggle would be the result of sensing that earlier in life we never succeeded in a similar quest with other significant sources of approval (parents, teacher, siblings, peers, etc.).

Paying attention to emotional reactions to current situations is important. Where and when, and with whom do we feel the most intense anger, frustration, anxiety, or depression?

How we behave under certain circumstances also provides crucial diagnostic data. A woman once told me that whenever she had an argument with her boss, she would go home and immediately overeat. What could such behavior tell her about how she thinks and feels in such a relational situation? What about the "workaholic" who becomes agitated when she is forced to do nothing, could she be following a rule such as, "To be approved, you must always be productive?"

What about other peoples' reactions to us - do we see any trends or themes there? A man complained that throughout his adult life people for some odd reason seem to be friendly for a while, but then eventually would withdraw from him. I might challenge such a fellow to ask what trends he might observe in his own behavior towards others. Could he be coming on too strong, demanding to be the center of attention when he is with them? If so, then what feelings and thoughts would probably underlie such attention-getting behavior? Perhaps a major *rule of approval* for him since childhood is that, "Unless you really work hard to make your presence known, others will ignore you."

Once we trace back to what are probably very significant *rules of approval,* we can ask where they must have come from originally. I tell my clients that the goal is not to dwell on the past, but to see how the past has influenced our lives to the present time. More correctly, we need to see how OUR INTERPRETATIONS of the past have continued to influence our relationship to ourselves, others, and ultimately to God Himself. One reason for investigating the roots of our rules of approval is to see that we were not born with them. They resulted from our childlike interpretation of the imperfect, sinful world around us. Knowing this can help us believe that God never intended for us to live with such rules.

Secondly, knowing that this was not God's intention, then we can be free to investigate what rules, if any, God does desire us to live by. Before we can do that effectively, we must first identify what human rules we have been driven by for so many years.

The Development of Shame

The awareness of having failed to fulfill significant "rules of approval" can be described by the word, "shame." In modern popular psychology, shame, or "toxic" shame is the current term for an inner sense of badness or inadequacy. It grows out of the negative interpretations made by a child, so that it is both a mindset and a corresponding feeling state. If one strongly believes that he is extremely unworthy, negative emotions will undoubtedly follow, which in turn will lead to some type of behavioral expression. As described earlier, the child's often distorted perception of reality, which places him or her at the center of his or her own universe, is coupled with inappropriate expectations from the adult world that result in abusive words and actions. Between these two factors, "shame-based" ideas arise within the mind of the child. For example, the child reasons that, "My father always seems to prefer spending his free time without me; there must be something basically wrong with me."

Shame attacks the very nature of our being. The child does not distinguish between her behavior and her worth as a person, but links the two together. Unfortunately, adults often do this as well. Even well meaning questions such as, "Have you been a good boy today?" can subtly give the impression that the relative appropriateness of the child's behavior is equated with the relative moral value of his whole self. If the child got in trouble that day, the implication would be, not only that his behavior was inappropriate, but also he himself was a "Bad Boy".

As a feeling state, shame is difficult to distinguish from guilt. An important and helpful distinction must be made between the two. Guilt focuses on the rightness or wrongness of our behavior, as well as the inner attitudes and motives from which it arises. Guilt says, "I have done something wrong", or "I have been very jealous towards my brother". Shame, in contrast, "goes the extra mile" and says, "Not only have I done something wrong, but that means there is something wrong with me!" "Not only did I make a mistake, but *I* myself must be a mistake...I don't deserve to be on this earth!" "Not only did I do something bad, but *I* must be bad!"

Shame, as we are now defining it, is not to be confused with the experience of "feeling ashamed." The question must be asked, of what are we feeling ashamed? Scripture makes it clear that right from the Garden of Eden, humans have felt "ashamed." Yet this sense of shame is directed towards sinful behaviors or attitudes. This type of shame is thus associated with the healthy guilt that God's Spirit uses to convict us of our sinful condition. However, while the Holy Spirit convicts us, He never condemns us as unworthy persons. Conviction of sinful attitudes and behaviors is, actually, the outpouring of God's gracious love towards us; since without an awareness of sin, it continues to destroy us. So, a healthy awareness of sin is ultimately liberating. It is then appropriate to feel "ashamed" of our sinful attitudes, motives and behaviors.

On the other hand, the process of shaming ourselves is devastating. The kind of shame we are now talking about causes us to "feel ashamed" about who we are, not just about our evil thoughts or actions. Having combed through Scripture for uses of the term "shame", I cannot find an instance in which the basic value, dignity, or worth of an individual is implicated. Unfortunately, we as human beings are capable of communicating this kind of shame to one another, and are capable of attributing it to ourselves. Many clients have related to me instances of wrongdoing in their pasts. Their frequent comment is, "I know God has forgiven me, but I cannot forgive myself." I explain that this lack of self-forgiveness is due to the sense of personal shame they have attached to their wrongdoing. We can feel forgiven for what we have done, or even what we have thought in our minds and felt in our hearts, but WE CANNOT FEEL FORGIVEN FOR WHO WE ARE.

Some may argue that since we are sinners, and sin is inherent in our very nature, then we *should* feel ashamed about *who we are*. True, but we are created in God's image and declared by God to be "very good" (Genesis 1:31). Our value and worth in God's eyes did not diminish when Adam and Eve sinned. When the Fall occurred, God did not say to Adam and Eve, "You have sinned *and* you are worthless." His message was instead, "You have sinned against Me, which is indeed a serious offense. You and your offspring will experience severe consequences; but the value I placed upon your being has not been diminished. In fact, I still love and value you so much, that I will provide a means of reconciling you back to Myself so we can have the intimate relationship that sin has broken." Thus, being sinners, and being in a chronically sinful state, does mar our relationship with God, but does not demean or minimize our value and worth as His creatures.

Shame leads us to make excuses for who we are. Probably the most striking definition of shame came from one woman I counseled who grew up in an intensely emotionally abusive home. She declared to me that she felt bad "for just living or breathing" in her household as a child. It was not a matter of whether her behavior met certain expectations; just her very existence had already in her young mind been condemned. This same woman, as an adult in my office, would frequently apologize to me for ideas she had and feelings she expressed, as if they were morally inadequate.

This phenomenon of shame is very powerful because it begins in the mind of a child. Like "*rules of approval*", it is maintained primarily on an unconscious level so that while the individual matures into adulthood physically and intellectually, shame-based thinking persists. The relationship between rules of approval and shame is this: We assume that if we do not fulfill certain rules, then we are unworthy; we are failures, etc. *Shame is the mindset and corresponding feelings that result from concluding that we must have failed to play by the rules*. Rather than questioning whether the rules are appropriate or not, we assume that our failure to fulfill the rules means that WE are inappropriate. The very essence of our personhood - our innate being, our value, dignity and worth as a human being - is, in our minds terribly scarred.

As stated earlier, failure to fulfill rules and the corresponding sense of shame leads to distorted perceptions in three areas --our view of ourselves, others, and ultimately God Himself. The person who struggles with intense self-hatred can only assume that other people will eventually reject him too, once they see how horrible he really is. This fear eventually is projected upon God Himself – "He will reject me, too." Remember, that since shame is largely maintained in our unconscious awareness, we can have theologically correct ideas about God as a loving, gracious Father, but our inner sense of shame actually steers us away from true intimacy with Him.

The "logic of shame" as it is applied to God works something like this: "*I was hurt, abused, mistreated, and neglected as a child. As far as God goes, there can only be two possibilities - Either he is not the all-loving, all-powerful Father that the Bible claims he is, and that would explain why he did not protect me from such shameful treatment. Or, he really is who he claims to be but apparently chose not to protect me. If that is the case, then such a wise, all-knowing God must have had a good reason: I MUST NOT HAVE DESERVED TO BE PROTECTED; I MUST HAVE DESERVED MY ABUSE, otherwise, an all-loving, and all-powerful God would have protected me.*"

We can easily understand how, as this logic persists into adulthood, even the professing Christian, at least on an unconscious level, feels terribly inadequate before God. Her only hope is now somehow to be "good enough" so that perhaps she can win a tiny portion of God's favor. Other people, of course, attack God's reputation. They consciously and deliberately state that God must not be trusted as who he says he is – "He has failed, not me." Yet, I find that when such hostility is directed at God, it is really a defensive maneuver to divert one's attention from the greatest shameful fear: "God is all right; I am the problem." I put it this way - *Shame always gets the last word.*

I observe the same dynamic when an extra-marital affair has occurred in a marriage. A husband cheats on his wife. When the truth is known, the wife can openly blame him for victimizing her. She can go as far as citing Scripture to justify her right to divorce him. However, while attacking the horrible evil on his part, such women have confided in me their deepest concern: "The fact that he found some other woman more desirable only confirms my sense of inadequacy. If I had been better somehow, he would not have been tempted in the first place." Now this wife, as in any marital conflict, would have been responsible for some of the conditions that arose in the relationship. Yet she is not responsible for the husband's choice to go outside the marriage as a "solution" to what he thought were the problems. However, the logic of shame, operating in the mind and feelings of the wife always gets the last word: "Even though I should be mad at him, I ultimately blame myself - I just am not worthy enough."

In the same manner, some people may speak very harshly on the surface towards God: "He failed me; he is not who he says he is...." The more hostile a person's attitude is toward God, the more we can be sure it is a diversion away from a deep sense of personal shame: "I am the problem - I am not worthy of God's favor as others seem to be."

Shame affects us in a way that we believe ourselves to be uniquely bad, even though we accept the theoretical fact that we are not alone. Survivors of childhood incest struggle with intense shame when a close family member, who, like God, is supposed to be loving and trustworthy, betrays them. They can then only conclude that they must be horribly deserving of the abuse. Many survivors have agreed with the prediction that I could take ten such survivors and gather them into a group. Each of them would assume that the other nine, no matter how much more horribly they were abused, are more worthy of God's love and grace than they are. Shame says, *"Not only are you bad, but you are uniquely scarred, more than anyone else."* This logic makes sense, remember, to the young "ego-centric" mind of a child. In the next chapter, we will learn more about the dynamics of shame and the ingenious ways we attempt to deal with our wounded sense of self.

Chapter Two:

Enslavement by Ourselves: *Hiding from Shame*

The phenomenon we have defined as "shame" becomes a powerful, life-driving force from childhood right into adulthood. Remember, however, that while we may refer to shame as "it", shame is not an independent entity with a life of its own. "It" is not like a virus that comes into our being from the outside to haunt us and create a type of disease. Rather, it is a kind of thinking style - a way of viewing reality; a means of interpreting what the world means to us and what our place is in the world around us. Since shame is a product of our own thinking - our own attempts to make meaning of our personal reality- then we do not have to work on changing the world around us as much as we do our own perceptions. Abusive people in the outside world have and can still attempt to shame us with verbal, physical or sexual attacks, but our inner sense of shame continues to come from our interpretations of these actions.

How we respond to criticism is indicative of how inner shame operates. First, a verbal criticism comes from someone other than, or outside of, us. We usually assume that our sense of hurt and anger is an automatic response to shaming words "entering" our being. It seems as if someone hurls a verbal arrow at us and it goes directly to our heart, or the seat of our emotions. In fact, what actually happens is that when the verbal missile comes at us, we make an internal, and usually unconscious, choice as to how we are going to receive or interpret the attack. There are several possibilities. We can, immediately and totally, accept the other person's assessment of us, ("I must be just as bad as this person says I am"). We can totally reject the other person's assessment of us, ("I am nothing at all like what they say"). Or we can take a more objective approach and think through whether there may be some truth in the criticism ("I don't like the way in which it was said, but if I am honest with myself, there is some truth in the statement").

In each kind of response, there is a filtering, or interpretive process going on inside of our mental computer. How we feel is a result of how we interpret the criticism. In the first two cases - either accepting totally or rejecting totally - there is a shame-based means of interpretation going on. In the first case, we unquestionably agree with the criticism, meaning that when someone shames us from the outside, we choose to shame ourselves internally in the same manner.

The second type of response, especially when done automatically, is a sign of defensiveness. If we deny the shaming criticism with great intensity, then it probably means that we also have chosen to believe it is true, but we do not want to face what we fear is true. Each of these responses on our part is the result of a shame-based way of thinking about ourselves. While it FEELS like others are attacking our sense of self directly, we are in fact intercepting their attacks and then agreeing with them.

This is precisely what a young child does who is the recipient of neglect and abuse coming from the external environment. A child does not have the capacity to make the third type of interpretive judgment which in essence goes like this – "Now, let me see,....this adult is telling me that I have failed to live up to certain expectations. As I consider these expectations, they really are not reasonable. So, the problem lies not with me, but with the external expectations and with those who are delivering them to me."

A child simply is not psychologically sophisticated enough and does not have enough experience yet in the world to take this type of more objective, non-shaming stance. As a result, kids virtually "absorb" shame. Yet the shame has entered in, only because the child, not being able to do otherwise, has agreed with the shameful signals from the outside. Actually, it is not fair to say that the child "chooses" to agree with the shame when he or she has no other option but to readily accept the negative messages. However, as time progresses, the child does continue to choose to agree whenever subsequent shaming experiences occur. As we will discuss later, it is a wonderful thing that a child makes choices, albeit unhealthy and inaccurate ones, because it means that no matter how badly a child has been abused and by whatever means, the capacity to choose has not been lost. It is this capacity that can be revived and can lead to the healing of inner shame and can clear the pathway for greater intimacy with God.

What *has* been lost, when a child receives shaming signals from the outside environment, is the child's awareness that he does not have to keep shaming himself every time similar signals appear. The child "chooses" to keep shaming himself every time others do, because he is not aware that he has the option to do otherwise. In a sense this is not a full, free choice, because the young child is not aware of the various options to choose from, especially a healthy perspective of one's self, even when others continue to shame.

The interplay between the human will, or our ability to choose, and the violation of our will through forms of victimization, is difficult to completely understand or express. It reminds me of the problem theologians have when they attempt to reconcile the notion of predestination, or God's choosing us to be one of his "elect", with the idea of human free will, which suggests that we choose God. I personally have given up a long time ago attempting to take sides on the issue. This appears to be one of those paradoxes in Scripture that is beyond our understanding; just as is the reality of Jesus Christ being fully human yet also fully divine.

In a similarly paradoxical manner, we are both victimized by other people's sinful choices towards us; *and* we end up making choices in response to our having been victimized. As Dr. Larry Crab says in his book, *Inside Out* (1988), we are both hurt and wounded people, but also "agents" of sin as well. This idea of agency means that while we suffer at the hands of others through no fault of our own, we also create some of our own ills. In other words, how we choose to respond to our hurt, pain, and shame is something for which only we are ultimately responsible.

The young child is clearly not responsible for external forms of abuse, whether they are verbal, physical, emotional, or sexual in nature. The young child is also not accountable for her initial acceptance of the sense of shame that results. In a sense, she is victimized by the limitations of her childlike perspective of herself and the outside world. However, as time goes on, the child does choose to continue interpreting forms of abuse and rejection as shaming. We can legitimately argue that the child's "choosing'" to shame herself is not a completely free choice based on an awareness of all the options. However, the point now is simply to recognize that an act of choice does occur, i.e., the child's human will has not been completely destroyed.

This process of choosing continues into adult life, primarily because it is hidden at a level below our conscious awareness. It is based on the original logic of a child who originally knew no better than to simply agree with the negative messages coming from others. Thus, the individual persists in interpreting relationships and life situations from this immature, shame-based logic, even though he grows up and matures in many other areas of life. He literally gets bigger physically, gains adult knowledge and skills, often including learning of Scriptural truths. Yet how the person relates to others, even God, is still determined by the hidden, shame-based logic of the immature child.

As grownups, we thus surprise ourselves when we speak, act, or feel in such a manner that defies adult logic about reality. I recall one man telling me that although he struggled in high school, he finally did so well in the military that he was selected for a high-level training program. Had he accepted the offer, he would not only have gone further in the military ranks, but would have had a very marketable skill in the civilian sector as well. Now, many years later, he was bemoaning his choice to decline the offer for further training, completely unaware of why he did so. In a similar fashion, many a female client has told me she cannot understand why she sabotaged a dating relationship with what appeared to be a rather mature, healthy young man, and instead married an immature man with a host of problems.

Examples such as these confirm that many choices we make during our adult lives are driven by logic of which we are not completely aware. It is also a shamed-basic logic, in that the choices we end up making always lead to an eventual self-confirmation that we really must be the unworthy person that we have feared being ever since childhood.

Now, having established the reality of shame's presence in our internal logic, let's next trace what we do with it. The inner thoughts and feelings associated with shame are so painful that we begin a lifelong process of responding to this pain in two major ways: We attempt to *cover it over* as best as possible, so we do not have to think about how horribly bad or inadequate we are and not feel the corresponding feelings. We also go about searching for ways to *compensate for* thinking so negatively about ourselves. In the remainder of this chapter, we will focus on the first of these two categories of response to shame.

THE ROLE OF ADDICTIONS: CATEGORY I:
"Covering Up"

Category #1 is a form of avoidance. The goal here is to distract ourselves from, or "cover up", the thoughts and corresponding feelings of self-hatred. From the "get go", as children originally sensing inner shame, we do our very best to avoid awareness of it. Forms of distraction are available to children, and they set the groundwork for what are in essence types of addictions. One definition of an addiction is any type of "mood altering" experience, or anything that we engage in to change the way we feel. Since the thinking or "logic" of shame is usually pretty well buried in the child's unconscious, the feelings are more of an immediate threat. A child may use television or modern video games to create such distraction, or may use other experiences such as play. The chosen form of addiction may not be harmful in itself to the child. The problem lies in the progressive dependence by the child upon the activity in order to dodge continually thoughts and feelings of shame.

Other forms of avoidance become available to the older child, teenager and adult. One 15-year old boy had recently completed a detoxification program for alcohol abuse when he was referred to me. After freely admitting that he simply switched to heavy use of marijuana upon returning home, he clearly stated that, "Basically, I don't want to feel anything." What he really meant, of course, was that he did not want to be aware of, in his case, not only the current turmoil in his family, but also his shameful sense of self associated with it. His logic of shame would have run something like this: "Not only have my parents had severe personal and marital problems for years, but since I am part of this family, there must be something inherently wrong with me also." This logic began a repetitive cycle of shameful feelings, leading to shame-based behavior such as school failure and quitting the school soccer team, a sport in which he apparently had significant skill. After sabotaging himself, each new experience of failure would only further convince him that he was indeed worthless, leading to more cycling between negative thoughts, feelings and behaviors.

The author of *Addiction and Grace* (1988), Gerald May, explains, "To be alive is to be addicted" (p.11). What we normally think of as addictions, (including chemicals such as alcohol or cocaine, but also experiences such as a gambling), are only the more obvious forms. In fact, we can be addicted to any experience, idea, or even other people (or I would add, their approval). God is the only object of our attention to which we cannot be addicted.

Incarcerated sexual addicts have told me that the actual experience of rape or pedophilia with a victim was not what drove them to their heinous crimes; instead, it was more the intense experience associated with planning out a crime, or stalking their victim. This process kept their minds and emotions on an experiential plane distinct from the awareness of inner shame from their own pasts as victims. The gambler will also tell you that the experience of winning is not the point. If it were, many would stop when they had won an amount significantly more than they had originally betted. Instead, it is the thrill of winning or losing, of "living on the edge", of going "double-or-nothing" just after you have won, that leads to gambling as a compulsive behavior. Teenagers call this heightened experience an "adrenalin rush."

I once saw an interview with a well-known millionaire, probably at the time one of the wealthiest men our country. He had just left his wife for a new girlfriend and was asked the obvious question by a reporter - "Why? You have everything - all the money you could want, a beautiful wife and family...." The man's immediate response succinctly states the addictive nature of his choice: "I have to have something exciting in my life at all times." In a similar fashion, a famous rock star who was abused as a child told an interviewer that performing before thousands of fans, is "the only time I feel alive." Finally, I once heard a racecar driver explain why he likes to drive so fast with the same exact words as the rock star.

A woman in my office once traced her pattern of overeating to situations of conflict. As an example, she explained how after an argument with her boss she would go home and raid the refrigerator. She was well aware that the experience of eating tasty food made her "feel better." This suggests another characteristic of the addictive process: Addictions all involve some means of control. In order to avoid the thoughts and feelings of shame, we must gain control of them by finding ways of distraction. A painful irony, however, is that as we try hard to control these noxious ideas and experiences, the very means we turn to end up seeming to over-control us. A person who turns to alcohol to control feelings of shame ends up feeling controlled by the chemical itself.

The same is true for the person who turns to gambling, sex, food, or even religious experience (to be distinguished from a true experience of God). Regarding the latter, a recovering alcoholic recently confessed to me, that at least for him, his longtime involvement in worship services that focused on "feeling God's presence", were just a form of "substitute addiction". This is not to say that particular worship styles are wrong biblically or are harmful psychologically, but I am referring to how the individual uses the experience.

Any therapist, and probably many pastors, will agree that some people seem to be addicted to chaos in their lives. While it is not done with conscious deliberation, certain individuals, couples, and entire families thrive on confusion, busyness, or over-commitment, and as a result are never quite able to finish what they have started. Just one example would be a family that has a host of its own problems already, feeling "led by the Lord" to take in a few foster children. Focusing on this new form of distraction would perpetuate a process of diverting attention away from some area of shame within an individual or within relationships.

I believe Christians can be "addicted" to the "busyness" of involvement in religious activity, including service in the church, personal devotions, Bible studies, helping others, etc. Such people, like "workaholics" outside of the church setting, are always avoiding something in their lives that signifies shame to them.

Consider the woman who "does everything" in church, but does it as a response to interpreting her husband's apathy towards their marriage as her fault because she is inadequate. Such a woman can eventually become controlled by her busyness; she just can't seem to say "No" to more opportunities for service.

In the same manner, a father and husband once admitted to me that he probably could be labeled a workaholic and alcoholic. His pattern was to stay at work as late as possible, which was easy since he ran his own business. Then he would go out to have a few "drinks with the boys", (what I call the "CHEERS bar mentality") and finally drag himself home about 9 p.m. every night. This lifestyle had developed in response to his belief that he had failed as a husband and father. Rather than feel the shame of this, as well as risk further shame, he buried himself in work and booze. However, by the time I had met him, he perceived himself to have been trapped by his own addictive lifestyle. He was no longer in control; his addictions seemed to control him.

Let's say a few more words about a concept mentioned above, that of "substitute addictions". The teenage boy, who "dried out" after heavy alcohol use, quickly turned to smoking pot. The large sand-filled bucket outside the church hall serves as an ash try for the nicotine-addicted attendees at Alcoholics Anonymous meetings. Former smokers admit to overeating, and addicts of all sorts have an experience of Christian conversion, but then can become "addicted" to religiosity, or the experiences offered to them in the religious community. All of these examples suggest that addictions are only symptoms. There is something greater going on at a deeper level of awareness and that is the logic and experience of shame. To seek a "cure" only for the addictive behavior or lifestyle itself, is to open the door for other forms of addiction, because the shame-base has been left untouched.

What happens to the recovering alcoholic who makes a sincere profession of faith, who joins a basically solid, Bible-believing church, but occasionally relapses into his addictive behavior? Imagine that he, with all good intentions, takes his struggle to a group of church leaders whom he respects and admires as representatives of God's power to heal. Imagine that such representatives, with sincere intentions, pray fervently and even lay hands upon this new believer. His initial response is to feel tremendously uplifted by the love and caring demonstrated by his Christian brothers.

While it is entirely possible for God to perform an immediate and total healing of this man's desire for alcohol, such an experience is quite rare. Otherwise, counselors like me would not be so busy. Instead, my best guess is that the experience of God's love, as demonstrated by the church leaders, does impress the man enough that he temporarily lays off the alcohol. He probably does sense that not only these men, but also God Himself loves him and desires that he relinquish his addictive behavior.

Yet it is only a matter of time before this attempt at recovery ends in a relapse. As soon as a renewed sense of shame is experienced, in any way, in any circumstance, this man could very easily revert to drinking as a means of "altering his mood". The problem, you see, is not that God's love is ineffective, or that the leaders or the man himself did not have enough faith, but rather that God's love affected this man only to the degree that he was aware that he needed it. In other words, the focus was only on the alcoholic behavior, and so completely ignored the underlying sense of shame. So in effect, he would have been temporarily "healed" from a symptom, meaning the addiction itself, but the cause of the real "disease" is beneath the surface of his awareness and that of the church leaders.

I am definitely not meaning to limit God's ability to heal in any way and at any time that He so chooses. However, I cite the above example, because while it happens to be hypothetical, I am sure that similar experiences are more the norm than are "instantaneous" healings. While I admittedly have not researched the topic thoroughly, I simply have never heard anyone testify to being completely healed of psychological symptoms such as anxiety or depression, which have gone on for years, by the instantaneous intervention of a "faith healer".

Perhaps, some have experienced the immediate "healing" from an addiction; but beware of the less obvious substitute addiction that would follow.

I do not doubt the genuineness of instantaneous healings when more physically based symptoms are involved. My best explanation for the difference between these, and what we might call more "psychologically based" problems, is that the latter involve an undiagnosed and thus untreated logic of shame in the individual's unconscious mind. My experience leads me to conclude that God's healing of shame and its symptoms (addictions) is a process that occurs over time, rather than instantaneously. It is the same process that the Apostle Peter recommends when he admonishes believers to "grow in grace" (II Peter 3:18). Many Christians quote the Apostle Paul's words in II Corinthians 5:17 which state, "If anyone is in Christ, he is a new creation; the old has gone, the new has come!" (NIV). The argument is that having had a "conversion experience", there is no need to consider one's previous history or life experiences as having any validity. The same argument is based upon Paul's declaration in Philippians 3:13b, 14 – "...Forgetting what is behind and straining towards what is ahead, I press on toward the goal to win the prize for which God has called me heavenward in Christ Jesus."

The argument for "forgetting our past" because it has no relevance suggests that only current behavior needs to be addressed. As long as we are not sinning in our deeds now, we are living the Christian life. So the alcoholic is told simply to quit drinking, or the incest survivor is told to stop withholding sexually from her husband. Simply change these behaviors and you will be back in God's good graces. This argument is formulated by taking the two above mentioned passages right out of their contexts. In the case of the Corinthian passage, the larger Biblical context strongly implies that the Christian life is a developmental process. We do begin and continue as "new creatures" in the sense that because Christ "covers" us with His righteousness, God now looks upon us "as if" we were righteous (cf. Galatians 3:27; Romans 4:7), and will treat us "as if" we are righteous, but not because we have actually become righteous. If the latter were true, we would no longer need Christ's "covering".

The Philippians passage must also be seen not only in the larger context of Paul's teaching and the teaching of the entire New Testament, but also in its immediate context. Paul has just finished arguing that what is no longer relevant is his long list of credentials as a well-educated and self-righteous Jew. That is the part of his history that he intends to "forget", because these credentials did not earn him a righteous status before God. Instead, some mistakenly assume that we are to forget everything in our pasts, including events, situations, and relationships that would have led to our inner logic of shame. Peter's strong admonition to "grow in grace" means that we progressively become more and more aware of our need for God's loving forgiveness and for Christ to be our "covering". We do not become immediately whole or perfectly righteous at the initial point of salvation. Because shame underlies our addictive behaviors, we do need God's Spirit to "grace" us with an increasing awareness of how this unhealthy logic drives us.

Chapter Three:

Enslavement by Ourselves: *Compensating for our Shame*

THE ROLE OF ADDICTIONS: CATEGORY #2 - "Compensation"

We also need the Spirit to illumine our awareness of the second major way in which we use addictions to respond to our shame. Regardless of how conscious we are of shameful thoughts and feelings about ourselves, our natural tendency is to make up for them somehow. We assume that if we work hard enough at it, we should be able to make ourselves good and thus be worthy of others' approval. The principle here is one of "equal and opposite reaction". The more shame we bear, the more we need to compensate in the direction of being very good. In fact, the ideal would be, of course, to achieve some state of perfection.

> SHAME > PERFECTION

I make the fundamental assumption that we are all "perfectionists" at heart. For most of my life, I have never considered myself to be a perfectionist, because in my mind, the term was reserved exclusively for those who are overly neat and organized, too fastidious, or what in professional circles we call "obsessive-compulsive". I'm talking about the super "neatnik" who can't leave the house until every inch of the place is clean, or the person who cannot leave their office at the end of a workday unless all her pencils are sharpened and placed in the same direction in her desk tray. I am thinking of the folks who have difficulty completing projects on time because they work at such a slow deliberate pace to avoid errors, yet what they do finally produce is virtually flawless, beautiful work.

While I could see some minor forms of such traits in myself, it has always been easier to spot them in others, especially in their exaggerated forms. It was, therefore, quite easy to dismiss any thoughts of myself as a perfectionist. The fact is, however, that God has placed in all of us, His creatures, an awareness of, and a natural desire for, a perfect state of affairs. I suspect this is an inner prodding of our soul or spirit towards God Himself, who is the only being who rightly can be described as perfect. Therefore, this God-awareness in the depths of our beings does create a movement towards the perfect, because as His creatures, we indeed have a propensity to move towards our Creator. Paul explains this to the Romans in Chapter 8, verses 22-23: "*We know that the whole creation has been groaning as in the pains of childbirth right up to the present time. Not only so, but we ourselves, who have the first fruits of the Spirit, groan inwardly as we wait eagerly for our adoption as sons, the redemption of our bodies.*"

Not only does the physical realm of creation long for ultimate perfection, but we also do so as spiritual beings. One way of summarizing the Gospel message is the following: "*Because Jesus Christ is perfect, we do not have to be.*" You see, being perfect, God has indeed set a standard of completion and flawlessness that He is not willing to compromise. In order for any being to enter His presence, one must be in a state of sinless perfection. The clear message of the New Testament states that Christ has provided the means for us to stand before God. Yet, we do so only because Christ functions as a perfect substitute for us, not because we could ever achieve perfection ourselves. Galatians 3:26-27 says, "*You are all sons of God through faith in Christ Jesus, for all of you who were baptized into Christ have clothed yourselves with Christ.*"

This image of being "clothed" with Christ refers to the fact that He covers our imperfect and sinful condition with His moral perfection, so that God now looks at us *as if* we are righteous, not because we actually are.

The problem we create for ourselves, however, is that rather than resting in this reality of Christ having been perfect on our behalf, we attempt to be perfect ourselves, and assume that others around us should be also. The result is a lifelong striving to be something we were never created to be. Not only are we inherently sinful, but we are also limited beings. We are not omnipresent (ever present) or omniscient (all knowing) as God is, yet we often expect ourselves to be. For example, how frequently do we blame ourselves for simple mistakes? By definition, a mistake is something that is unintentional, and is the result of our lack of total awareness. If I schedule two clients for the same hour, I certainly do not do so on purpose. Rather, whenever I have made such an error, it is due to the fact that my mind can only concentrate on so many bits of data at once. My thinking becomes overloaded, so I cannot attend perfectly to all the information that I am attempting to be in control over. If I brow beat or shame myself for such mistakes, I must be assuming that I should have unlimited mental capacity and total awareness of everything in my mind!

The notion of perfection can be understood to have several components. Since God is the only Perfect Being, we can look to His nature as revealed in Scripture to understand just what it means to be perfect. First, God is *morally* perfect. He would fail to be God if he violated any of His own standards of right and wrong (whereas pagan gods often commit immoral acts in human mythologies). God is Good in every sense of the Word, which includes the fact that he is perfectly *loving.* God is also *self-sufficiently* perfect. He is perfectly complete in and of Himself. He did not create humankind because He needed us to fulfill his sense of happiness by worshipping Him, or to provide companionship for Him. No, the only sense in which He "needed" us would be that because He is *perfectly loving*, He did require someone to love. Being *perfectly powerful*, God chose to create us, and a world for us to enjoy, because His perfectly loving nature naturally moved Him to share His love with others.

Thus, God is perfectly good, loving, self-sufficient, powerful, and also *perfectly sovereign.* This means that not only was He in control of everything before and at the point of creation, but He continues to be so throughout all eternity. He never loses total control over the reality He creates. Implicit in God's sovereignty is the fact that He is *all-knowing.* Nothing has every happened, nor ever will, that escapes His awareness and His Will. God never "messes up". He never makes a mistake. He is flawless in all His thoughts, feelings and actions. It is often in these same respects that we as humans desire to be perfect. We would like to be totally in control of all life's circumstances, for ourselves, and often for others. What parent has not wished that they could control every thought, feeling and action of their child to guarantee some idealized outcome for their life? How often do we desire to perform perfectly in any task that we might perform? Wouldn't we like to have total knowledge and awareness of all truths, to be fully aware of the future, to have unlimited power over the physical world, etc.?

I would summarize all these aspects of perfection by suggesting that God is both *unlimited* (infinite) and *flawless*. In contrast, we are both limited (finite) creatures (not self-sufficient, not omniscient, and not omnipotent) and flawed (morally defective). If we could perform in an unlimited and flawless manner all the time, then we, like God, could be morally perfect, completely self-sufficient, and totally in control of ourselves and the world around us.

Yet to aim for such a goal is by definition impossible, leading to the awareness that we are indeed *finite and flawed.* Rather than accepting our limitations as created beings, we shame ourselves for not being God (an attitude that God never takes towards us, because He never intended for us to be perfect as He is). As stated earlier, the more shameful we feel about ourselves, the more we assume that we can and should achieve some state of perfection in order to compensate for our inadequacies. Both my sense of shame and my drive for perfection are predominantly buried in my unconscious, so I naturally tend to deny that any of this applies to me. However, I strongly believe this process of compensation, or "proving myself," is a continual one for all of us. My inner sense of shameful inadequacy leads naturally to a desire to not only cover up such threatening thoughts and feelings, but also make up, or compensate, for them. The ideal state would be for me to function as a perfect flawless being.

Shame and our corresponding drive for perfection are "all or nothing" phenomena. Our reasoning is that in order to pull ourselves out of a shameful state, we must be more than good; we must be completely, totally, perfectly intact as human beings. By definition, one cannot be "a little bit perfect". Either we are perfect or we are not. Not being perfect equals total inadequacy or unworthiness. This extremely dichotomous logic sets us up for automatic failure. To compensate for shame, we attempt to be perfect, which, being an impossible goal, we are doomed to fall short of. The result is a greater sense of shame, creating an endless, addictive cycle of shame...attempts at perfection...sense of failure...more shame...more attempts at perfection.

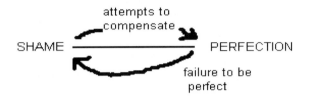

This is the cycle, I believe, that underlies all addictions. Let's take two types as examples. First, consider forms of substance abuse. The alcoholic or cocaine addict has some subjective sense of shame, stemming, as with all of us from childhood. Somehow, he never has measured up in life, so has assumed that he must prove himself to a perfect extent in some specific area or areas of life. Let's say he decides to be a very successful businessman to prove to his demanding father that he can "make it" on his own. As he enters adulthood, he makes valiant attempts, but never quite feels like he has achieved his goal. This lurking sense that no matter how hard he tries, it is not good enough (because it isn't perfect), is too uncomfortable to live with. Alcohol then becomes the means of numbing his feeling and thinking state so that he is not aware of his sense of failure.

Another addictive cycle begins with the introduction of a chemical substance: the alcoholic drinks to cover over shame, then eventually he sobers up, only to realize how the alcohol is ruining his life (probably his business and his relationships). This realization engenders more self-hatred, which in turn leads to further drinking, etc....

A second case could be that of the workaholic. He attempts to compensate for his internal sense of shame by earning more and more money and climbing higher and higher up the corporate ladder. As long as he senses that he is on an upward swing, he may avoid the numbing effects of substances. However, the experience of working hard, focusing always on how much more there is to do, distracts his mind and feelings away from shame. Japanese businessmen who die instantly in the midst of the "high" of perpetual 18-hour days are actually addicted to the emotional and mental state of intense stress. Like any other form of addiction, including chemical, the workaholic feels more normal while engaging in the addictive behavior than when not, even though the addiction is killing him.

The workaholic is never satisfied because he has not yet achieved some state of perfection, and, of course, never will. Our point here, though, is that underlying all forms of addiction - those that we use primarily to cover over shame, those that we use primarily to compensate for shame, and those that do both - is a more fundamental addiction to perfection itself. Just as the alcoholic says she MUST have a drink, or the workaholic says he MUST keep working harder, so shame says we MUST be perfect. However, an important note must be made here. Perfection is not the final goal of our strivings. Rather, it is the means to the ultimate end of **approval**: *We assume that could we reach perfection, then others would finally approve of us, and THEN, we could finally approve of ourselves.* The shame-based voice from childhood, which says we have never been good enough, continues to haunt us right through adult life. To silence this voice, we attempt to either cover it over, and/or prove it wrong by assuming we must be virtually perfect in at least some, if not all areas of life.

My life operates according to the clock. As a psychologist who often sees clients hour after hour, I am all too aware of how many hours I have done at a given point during the day, and how many more appointments I have to go before quitting time. Also, as a person who prides himself upon being competent and doing what I consider to be "good work", I am cognizant of my desire to avoid any indications of failure. A while ago, I found myself taking comfort in the fact that if I somehow perceived myself to have failed before the day was over, then I could excuse my failure because of my hectic schedule. That is to say, that hard work and long hours naturally breeds fatigue, and as a day or week progressed, any hint of failure could easily be explained by my increased tiredness.

While observing myself to have engaged in such reasoning, I realized that I was developing what could be considered as a type of "alibi". In a legal context, an alibi is a plea that the accused was somewhere else at the time of the crime being investigated. If such an alibi is accepted by the court, then the accused is acquitted, and he need not pay the legal consequences. Outside of the criminal setting, the term "alibi" simply means an excuse. In my own case, I found myself using the prospect of fatigue as an alibi for any signs of potential failure in my role as a psychotherapist. More precisely, since I had not actually yet failed at the time I engaged in this reasoning, I was using fatigue as a potential alibi, or what I call an *"alibi in the back pocket"*. I did not actually need such an excuse at the precise moment, but anticipating the possibility of failure, I could immediately bring the alibi of fatigue "out of my back pocket" if it was indeed needed.

Now in the criminal case, a certain standard is being applied. Either the accused did, in fact, commit the crime, or the opposite is true - the accused is not guilty. Either the defendant passes or he fails. Without an adequate alibi, the facts would argue that the accused did violate a standard of justice and would therefore deserve just punishment. Well, I too had been measuring myself against a particular standard of performance in my counseling with couples, individuals, and families. For me, however, the standard by which I would be graded "pass" or "fail", "guilty" or "innocent", was not as clear in my own mind as are the standards of the written civil law. Nonetheless, I was operating with such a standard in my mind, even if it lay dormant in the parts of which I am less conscious.

What specific form would "passing" or "failing" take in my case? The more I contemplated this question, the more I realized how closely my standards of performance approximated the level of perfection. Perhaps one slight comment on my part that did not sound absolutely profound, or an error in scheduling, or forgetting the name of a client's spouse, or ...on and on and on. I think I was mostly guarding myself against some signal from a client that I had not been virtually flawless in my attempts to counsel them.

Now, of course, such standards are not only overly ideal and unrealistic, but they also reflect a degree of arrogance and egotism on my part to presume that I could ever achieve them. Yet this is precisely why I need an alibi. I have set standards for myself that are impossible to fulfill. Therefore, in order to live with myself, to not perceive myself as a complete failure, I create an excuse for not holding myself accountable for being less than perfect – "I'm too tired; I have too many clients already this week; people put too many demands upon me as it is," etc. So, I blame somebody or something else for my "failure".

Whenever I discover such humbling truths about my own inner attitudes and motives, my usual first response is to try to deny them further. Experience has taught me however, that God's Spirit is tenacious in His desire for me to see myself as I really am. Eventually, I give in and accept the fact that not only do I use such alibis, but also I do so because I expect perfection of myself. I then begin to wonder if the people I work with also use their own forms of alibis to "save face" when they fail to achieve their own perfect standards.

Chapter 4:

Our Response to Shame: *The Mountain of Perfection*

I like to illustrate what has been said to this point with the image of a tall mountain, the peak of which would symbolize some perfectionistic ideal. One category of persons, whom I call *"**mountain-climbers**"*, attempts to avoid their sense of shame (fearing that they will be stuck at the bottom of the mountain) by frantically scaling the steep slope with hopes of getting to the top. Yet, because the final goal is perfection, one never actually reaches the top, so the climb is endless. Thus, the workaholic can never be fully satisfied with the amount or quality of work. There is always more to be done. The homemaker can never clean the house enough, or the people-pleaser can never gain enough approval.

Aware of this process within himself, one of my clients once amended my diagram by stating that his mountain actually has no peak - it just rises up forever into the clouds. In his very entertaining book entitled, *A Walk In the Woods* (1998), author Bill Bryson chronicles his adventures while hiking the Appalachian Trail. The following quote about a literal "mountain climber" helps illustrate the figurative mountain climber as well:

> The hardest part was coming to terms with the constant dispiriting discovery that there is always more hill. The thing about being on a hill, as opposed to standing back from it, is that you can almost never see exactly what's to come. Between the curtain of trees at every side, the ever-receding contour of rising slope before you, and your own plodding weariness, you gradually lose track of how far you have come. Each time you haul yourself up to what you think must surely be the crest, you find that there is in fact more hill beyond, sloped at an angle that kept it from view before, and that beyond that slope there is another, and beyond each of those more still, until it seems impossible that any hill could run on this long. Eventually you reach a height where you can see the tops of the topmost trees,

with nothing but clear sky beyond, and your faltering spirit stirs – nearly there now! – but this is a pitiless deception. The elusive summit continually retreats by whatever distance you press forwards, so that each time the canopy parts enough to give a view you are dismayed to see that the topmost trees are as remote, as unattainable, as before. Still, you stagger on. What else can you do? (p.35)

The best that a *mountain-climber* can hope to attain is to reach a certain peak, and revel temporarily in his or her achievement. Soon, however, the drive to continue on to higher peaks kicks in, and the climber is off again, demanding further accomplishments. Thus, the businessman who does finally become salesman of the month, then feels compelled to strive for even greater heights within the company. Likewise, the student who achieves all A's at the end of a semester, takes a well-deserved break. She then heads back to class, stating to herself that she must therefore do as well, if not even better, the next semester, the next year, and so on.

The problem for the *mountain-climber* is that the mountains of life keep getting higher and higher, and/or more numerous. Our traveler in the *Introduction,* Alice, kept demanding more and more of herself as she moved from the role of student to spouse and mother. Eventually, she crashed due to sheer exhaustion: Too many balls to juggle in the air all at once.

Some may ask, "What's wrong with setting higher and higher goals for ourselves – shouldn't we always be trying to improve at whatever we do?" My response is that there is nothing wrong with setting goals and continually improving our skills or level of performance; the error comes when we assume that our basic value and worth is dependent upon such perpetual success. In addition, when our ultimate goal is perfection, we have no option other than eventual burn-out, since God has not designed us to achieve a state of flawlessness. We are limited and flawed creatures, whether we like it or not.

The second category of persons I have come to call *"base-campers"*. These folk, often labeled "lazy" and "irresponsible", look up from the base of the mountain and determine that since the peak is unattainable, it is not even worth attempting to climb. In fact, they would rather take the "rap" for doing nothing than to try their hardest and fail. Here's where the notion of **alibis** comes in: "Since I expect perfection of myself, I can either 'go for it' and risk failure, or avoid failure by not risking at all". The *mountain-climbers* often avoid risk of perceived failure by using alibis that explain why they didn't give their best effort. The *base-campers* use alibis to avoid trying at all. Our greatest fear is that if we try our best, our best won't be good enough; and if good enough means perfection, then we're all in trouble. We all need alibis.

Several years ago, I heard an internationally ranked figure skater admit on national TV that she had been afraid to work her hardest, because she might not end up with first prize. Being aware of this, she was now trying to be content with her own "personal best" effort, whether she always was the victor or not. Shortly after that interview, she was injured off the ice, just prior to the Olympic Games. No one, including herself, expected her to even compete in the Olympics, let alone win a medal. Her injury, however, provided a very tangible alibi. She went out and tried her best, subconsciously realizing that she would suffer no shame if she failed slightly or profoundly. This alibi allowed her actually to "let out all the stops" which resulted in one of her best performances ever.

A "base-camper's" alibi could consist of his or her own negligence. A student who ideally has A+ standards reports that he should have studied harder for the final exam rather than staying out late with friends the night before. Such individuals attempt to fool themselves into lowering their standards, so as not to experience too much disappointment and shame: "I never really wanted to make the basketball team anyway; I have better things to do with my time." In fact, such a young person would probably "sabotage" himself by quitting team try outs before the final cut was made, or perhaps by not even going out for the team at all.

Another set of alibis can be directed at other people or external forces. The "dog ate my homework" approach has its many counterparts amongst adults who avoid responsibility for their own actions when they are afraid that their efforts will fall short of perfection. Alcoholics are well known for their irresponsibility in many areas of life, not just drinking. The alcoholic husband blames his wife for not keeping the kids under control, so that he is "forced" to drink, and then blames his boss for firing him when his repeated tardiness to work is due to suffering hangovers.

Many will actually accept labels that correspond to being a *base-camper* rather than risk experiencing the perception of total worthlessness that results when one cannot be perfect. Imagine the chronic alcoholic who has denied having a problem for many years, in spite of the prayers and efforts of his wife and others to break through his denial. Finally, one day, his buddies convince him to go to an Alcoholics Anonymous meeting and the light dawns on him. He returns jubilantly to his wife, announcing that he now knows he is an alcoholic, and frankly, AA isn't so bad after all: "There are plenty of guys just like me." His wife is overjoyed for the first several weeks. Eventually, she ventures the question, "Honey, I'm so glad you've been getting help with your drinking problem. But, now do you think you could at least begin looking for a job again after not working for five years?" The husband stares back at her in disbelief. She continues, "What's wrong?" He simply responds, "I can't go back to work - I'm an alcoholic!"

For this fellow, the *label* of "alcoholic" becomes a convenient means of avoiding responsibility. Why such avoidance? Because his underlying thinking involves the shame-perfection cycle: "If I attempt to work, I would have to succeed perfectly. I'm too afraid my best effort will not be good enough, so I best not try at all." In a similar fashion, I once had a woman come to me and virtually beg that I diagnose her with "Manic-Depressive Illness" (now more commonly called "Bipolar Illness"). Her understanding of this label was that it referred to some condition beyond her control, and she all but admitted that then her family could not hold her accountable for her irresponsible behavior.

The shame-perfection logic leads one even to admit responsibility for poor choices ("I should have studied more consistently throughout the semester rather than cram for final exams"), as well as to search for conditions that are not one's fault. Regarding the latter, I will go so far as to say that any situation in life (being an abuse victim), a medical condition, and any psychiatric condition could be used as an alibi, to avoid the sense of shameful failure. This is not to suggest that the individual causes such things as childhood abuse, medical illness, or even some emotional or mental problems. No, what I am suggesting is the notion that any such situations or conditions can be used as excuses or alibis. Shame-based logic leads us to blame external conditions (e.g., abuse from others), and those we would like to think are external (e.g. having the 'disease' of alcoholism or depression), so that we do not have to see ourselves as failures.

As I have just intimated, I believe that most "psychiatric conditions" cannot be reduced totally to "chemical imbalances" as many of my clients have been led to believe. The jury is still out as to what originally causes forms of depression and various anxiety states. Undoubtedly, chemical changes do occur in such "conditions", but why should we assume a cause-and-effect relationship? A Biblical perspective of human nature certainly is not what some have called "biologically reductionistic." Scripture portrays us as being ultimately very responsible for our thoughts, feelings, and behaviors; whereas the biological reductionism assumes that neurochemical dysfunction is to blame for any imperfect functioning.

The mind-body relationship is very complex, and I do not discount the influence of physical states upon thinking, feeling, and behaving. I am just concerned that we avoid personal responsibility when we see ourselves as having a "condition" that is totally beyond our control. A prime example is the increasingly popular diagnosis of "Attention Deficit Disorder" (ADD). Once thought to be only a problem for pre-adolescent children, primarily boys, our field has now extended the diagnosis to males and females, children, adolescents and adults. The general public has swallowed the myth that this is a predetermined, biologically based condition over which one can only gain control through psychotropic medication. Like most other psychiatric diagnostic categories, the label "ADD" only refers to a set of symptoms, the causes of which are not yet completely clear. Until when and if a test, or a combination of tests, is able to clearly prove a direct cause-and-effect relationship between brain dysfunction and these symptoms, we need to be careful how we portray this to the public. To date, such evidence has not been offered by the psychiatric community, yet people are repeatedly told that they have this "condition", the implication being that it is precisely like diabetes or cancer which can indeed be more clearly diagnosed.

The real issue, however, is not whether such "conditions" with medical-sounding labels are neurochemically-caused or not. The greater concern is that people understand themselves to have "something" that is not their fault. This allows them to excuse themselves for imperfect functioning, thus avoiding the experience of shame. Even for those who have been affected by external causes (as we all have to some degree), such as the sexual abuse victim, it is tempting to hold onto to a "victim identity". This is exemplified by people who attend support groups (and we now have groups for survivors of all kinds of life situations), but never seem to truly recover, thus becoming in a way addicted to the group and the label itself. Why?

Well, it is easier to admit that we have a chronic problem, or will always be "in recovery" than to face the reality that without any such excuses, we are free to try to be perfect. Such freedom, without alibis is terrifying, because we know we can never be perfect, which must mean we are the opposite - worthless. So, we'd rather hold onto any label we can.

One other variation on this same theme is the following: Some of us will even accept labels attached to our own behavior or poor judgment, such as the student who did not plan well throughout the semester. This seems preferable to having had no reason but to try our best, but find out our best is not good enough. You see, shame attacks the very core of our being - our basic sense of self - not our behavior itself. We would rather bear a label attached to our behavior than admit that we are inadequate (less than perfect) in the very core of our being. As a result, being a *base-camper* is not so bad. I can even joke about it to others. Then they will expect less of me and I of myself. Without the label, I would have no excuse but to be perfect, which is impossible, so I would have to face my sense of shame.

While the *mountain -climbers* and *base-campers* look like polar opposites, they are driven internally by the same perfectionistic strivings.   In addition, these categories are not completely dichotomous in that an individual can vacillate between one or the other. After a while, the climber gets too weary and falls back down on the couch (often expressed through psychological symptoms involving anxiety and depression, and their physical manifestations). Eventually, he gets up to try the mountain again, only to fall back in exhaustion at some other point in the future.

The crux of the problem, therefore, lies not in the alibis themselves, but the unrealistic and perfectionistic ideals which necessitate their creation in the first place. If I stop attempting to be perfect, then I no longer need an alibi to explain why I can't be perfect. Yet our underling sense of shame, which we all bear to some degree or another, insists that we MUST be perfect or we are unworthy of the approval of others, or God Himself, and thus unworthy of self-approval.

This, then, is the means via which we enslave ourselves: having been enslaved by the shaming effects of the imperfect and sinful world around us, so that we learn as children to view ourselves as unworthy, we now come up with ways to "earn our salvation" by both covering over and compensating for our loathsome condition. While others had originally victimized us, we now as adults attempt as Dr. Crabb and others have said in their own words, to "heal ourselves." Ultimately, we become more enslaved by these self-generated solutions to our problem of shame, than by the shame itself or its original sources. In Part II of this book, we will learn how a deepened dependence upon God and His grace can free us not only from our "dysfunctional" pasts, but also from our attempts to save ourselves: thus begins the "Pathway to Freedom."

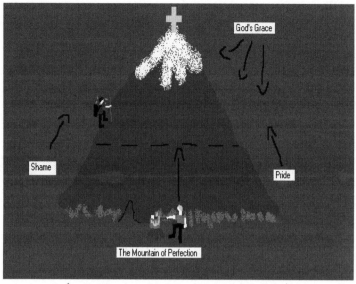

(computer drawing by Jenna Mae Sweitzer)

IDENTIFYING MY STRIVINGS FOR PERFECTION

The key to a more precise understanding of what may be your own unique "mountains of perfection" is to begin the process of investigation prayerfully. Ask God to reveal to you the areas in your life in which you feel compelled to achieve ideal or perfect standards. As we will see further, such strivings hinder our growing closer to God. If we pray such a prayer with a sincere and humble heart, He will indeed answer, perhaps not instantly, but He does want us to be aware of anything that keeps us from relationship with Him.

Stand back from yourself and begin with two categories of questions.

First, when and under what circumstances do I react with most intensity? For example, when do I become most frustrated or angered? This will give clues to what you are most striving for. If you react with **extreme defensiveness** to criticism from your spouse about how you relate to your kids, perhaps one of your "mountains" involves being the "perfect parent". If you become very angry when you are interrupted while working on a project, how important is it to you to complete the job in a perfect time frame or a perfect manner?

Related to this is the observation of *how I spend my time*. What do I focus my energies on the most and why do I work so hard? Of course, we should have strong passions in life, for both work and play. The question is how much we attempt to gain approval through perfect performance.

The other category of questions involves the opposite approach to life, i.e., *avoidance*. Rather than striving towards some goal, what are activities, situations, or even people whom I most desire to avoid? Do I find myself *making excuses* to myself or to others as to why I cannot be involved in certain situations? The person who attends Sunday worship service, but never the adult Bible classes that precede the service, may fear the shame that could come from being biblically illiterate: "What if I am asked to look up a passage of Scripture when I don't know which end of the Bible is up?" Such a person, never having had the opportunity to study Scripture seriously, would assume that he should have some innate perfect and total knowledge of the Bible, something that no one else would ever expect of him. However, to avoid a sense of shameful failure, he would rather not go near a situation in which his imperfections would be exposed.

Ask God to reveal to you not only what situations you might avoid, but also what your underlying motives are. Chances are good that you actually expect virtual perfection of yourself in terms of knowledge, skills, or talents. Since you expect perfection of yourself, but know you could never achieve it, you would prefer to avoid the situation altogether rather than do your best and find out it is not good enough.

Additionally, *indecisiveness* and *lack of commitment* are indicators of the "base camper" approach. In both cases, there is a fear of making the wrong, or less than perfect, response. I once counseled a man who admitted to asking his wife if she would like to go to a movie and then forcing her to choose which one. Why? Well, if either one or both of them did not like the movie, it would not be his fault, but hers!

Closely related is the very common problem of *procrastination.* This makes a convenient alibi, because even if we never verbalize it to ourselves or others, we know down deep that if whatever we try to accomplish does not turn out perfectly, we can chalk it up to having waited to the last minute. Like the chronic alcoholic, we are willing to accept "the rap" for being a procrastinator, rather than taking the risk that our best effort is not perfect.

Keep in mind that some of us lean more in the direction of the *mountain-climber* approach, and others in the direction of the *base-camper* approach. However, rarely is it the case that we function exclusively in one category or the other. Remember, these two terms, "mountain-climber" and "base-camper" describe not individuals or groups of people, but rather two styles of approaching the problem of perfectionistic ideals.

My sense is that the vast majority, if not all of us, exhibit combinations of these styles. I referred earlier to a gentlemen who worked long hours in his own business, and then would stop off late at night for a few drinks with his buddies at the local pub, and finally return home, only to hear his wife's frustrations from a day of dealing with unruly teenagers. He admitted to me that he often worked longer (mountain-climber) and hung at the bar (base-camper) in order to avoid a sense of failure as a husband and father. He stated that he once tried to be "good" husband and father, but when I probed further, what I really heard were expectations that could be translated thusly: "Whenever I say 'jump,' my teenagers should immediately reply, 'How high?' and "My wife should always agree with everything I say." Notice the perfectionist expectations of his family, which, of course, reflect those of himself – "I must be such a perfect husband and father that my family responds perfectly." To avoid the shame of perceived failure, he admitted to using both workaholism (mountain climber) and alcoholism (base-camper) as alibis. He also would shift responsibility to his wife: "When I get home late from work, and my wife complains that the kids are unmanageable, I can remind her that she has been with them all day, and hence she has failed."

I would add yet one more example of combining mountain-climber and base-camping approaches. I call this the "*perpetual chaos*" style. Some folks always seem to be biting off more than they can chew in their lives, shooting for mountain peaks that are way beyond their abilities or time constraints, or perhaps are perpetually attempting to climb more than one mountain at a time. An example would be the woman who was struggling daily with her own depression (due to a history of childhood abuse), an unsatisfactory marriage, and a seriously disturbed young son. At the end of one counseling session, she asked as she exited the office, "I've been thinking of taking in a foster child – what do you think, Dr. Sweitzer?"

A college student may repeatedly take on too many courses and/or too many difficult ones in a given semester; a man may join too many church committees, in addition to his more than full-time job; a therapist may take on too many clients in a given week. In all of these cases, the intense "mountain-climber" approach of doing too much serves in itself as an alibi: *"If I fail to live up to my perfectionistic expectations, then I can always admit to myself or others that I probably was trying to do too much at once."* This admission, however, would be preferable to setting a more reasonable pace for ourselves, and then failing to achieve perfection and having to face the shameful awareness that we alone, without any excuses, are not "good enough."

As you observe your own life, look for areas in which you attack too intensely, but also areas in which you avoid. Chances are good that you will find some in each category. In humility, ask God to reveal to your awareness what your unrealistic expectations may currently be in your life roles, which style you use in various situations, and what your corresponding alibis must be.

PART TWO:

THE PATHWAY TO FREEDOM:
JESUS CHRIST AS OUR "PERFECT ALIBI"

Chapter Five:

Freedom from Others: *Healing our Shame*

There are two main forces that drive us towards our individual "peaks of perfection." The first has been dubbed, by popular psychology, as "shame" or "toxic shame." The second is what we can call good old-fashioned human pride, which we will deal with in Chapter 6. For now, let's examine the question of how does one go about becoming free from shame: "How can I become healed from the painful wounds to my sense of self which remind me that I am "worth less" than others are?"

Entire volumes have already been written by both those in and outside of the realm of Christian psychotherapy about this healing process. The majority of them focus on the need to identify false beliefs about ourselves that originally developed in childhood and have persisted into adulthood. In this "cognitive" approach to dealing with problems, the client is encouraged to put into words the unhealthy, demeaning statements that they have developed over the years. Examples would be ideas such as, "I am worthless...not good enough...unable to succeed...a loser...shameful...bad...undeserving of love...," and many variations on such themes. The basic cognitive model states that the way we think affects the way we feel, and the way we feel determines how we behave. Our behaviors eventually elicit responses from other people, which we, in turn, interpret as proof of our original shame-based beliefs.

To illustrate this process, let's revisit our highly "paranoid" friend, Frank, taking the risk to attend a church service. He nervously slinks into a back pew, perhaps a few minutes after the service has begun, to avoid drawing attention to himself. He begins with the assumption that others will not like him, as has seemed to be the case in the past, ultimately because he is fundamentally inadequate, flawed, and unlovable. Simply put, the man who does not like himself, is going to make the leap of logic to "others will therefore not love or like me either." So, our nervous friend sits tensely through the church service, but as time progresses, he decides maybe this isn't so bad after all. No one treats him unkindly. In fact, during a greeting period, people around him shake his hand and welcome him, exchanging first names. At the conclusion of the service, the pastor announces that there will be a "coffee hour" in Fellowship Hall – all are invited for a time of refreshment and fellowship.

Normally this would be too threatening for our skittish friend, but given the warmth he experienced during the service, he convinces himself that it is worth a try – maybe this group of people is different, and maybe they will not notice his inner sense of shame and inadequacy. As he enters Fellowship Hall, he notices small groups of people huddled in two's and three's chatting excitedly while imbibing coffee, tea, and cookies. Our friend gets in line for his own goodies, and once he procures them, he suddenly realizes he does not know where to go next – "I don't know these people; I can't just go up and join one of these groups…" A wave of anxiety propels him to head for the corner of the room, find a lonely chair, drink his coffee and eat his cookies while avoiding eye contact with anyone who might happen to see him.

Meanwhile, a few parishioners pause in their conversation long enough for one of them to glance over to the corner and see our friend sitting rigidly all by himself. She turns to her friends and states, "Oh, there's that man who came into the service by himself today; he must be feeling uncomfortable all by himself. Shame on us for not noticing him sooner and inviting him to join us. Let's go over and introduce ourselves." Our friend looks up just in time to see these folks huddled in conversation while looking his way. Alarm signals immediately blare in his psyche! "Oh, no, they're talking about me…and now they are headed in my direction." Before they can even get close, he leaves his half-drunk cup of coffee on the floor, and makes a "bee-line" for the rear exit -- never to be seen again in that church.

The progression, you see, begins with his initially ingrained, shame-based belief, that he is fundamentally flawed and inadequate. This naturally produces the assumption that others will also think of him this way and treat him accordingly (i.e., rejection). This thinking leads to the emotion of fear and anxiety, culminating in avoidant behavior. When others observe his withdrawal (e.g., hiding off by himself), they naturally react with some puzzlement and confusion, but in fact their attitude towards him may be one of love and concern. He then interprets their reaction towards him as proof positive of his initial shame-based assumptions – "See, they're coming after me; they think I'm weird." Finally, this interpretation leads to more anxiety and the need to flee – "I'm out of here..."

The entire cycle creates one big self-fulfilling prophecy. Underlying shameful beliefs about ourselves eventually lead to a solidification of such ideas and the corresponding increase in shame-based behavior and intensification of negative emotions. This occurs in more than one way, as we will see later. Certainly one powerful illustration of this principle is this closed cycle of logic, that begins and ends with shame-based beliefs about ourselves.

I have entitled this chapter, *Freedom from Others: Healing Our Shame,* but I want to underscore a very important fact here. The unhealthy expectations of others may have been the original source of our shame, but we all develop our own perfectionist expectations of ourselves in response to that shame. Since such standards are unattainable, just like the paranoid fellow above, we continually recreate our sense of shame by repeated failure to be perfect. It has been correctly stated by other authors that we are more victimized by our responses to the past than we are by the past itself.

This is a hurdle of self-awareness that is often difficult for my clients to grasp. Everyone who comes in my door (and every other human being who never will) has some story to tell regarding **external shame**. Other people have ignored, manipulated, victimized, abused, abandoned or rejected us. Each of us has been hurt in someway, intentionally or not, by other imperfect and sinful people somewhere in our life histories. In no way do I want to minimize the significance of these personal experiences. I have heard many tragic stories, as all counselors do, some of which are so traumatic that just listening to them can negatively affect the counselor's own soul. I will address this issue of traumatic experiences in a while. However, first, I want to emphasize that **we** are responsible for the unrealistic demands *we* *place upon ourselves* in response to others' shameful behavior towards ourselves.

I may be counseling a man who takes great pains to explain to me that no matter how hard he has tried for 20 years, he cannot live up to his wife's expectations of him.   In some cases, I never have the opportunity to meet the spouse, but I do not need to in order to help this man.   Let's say that during his own childhood, this man was unable to win his father's approval, and as any child would, he learned to blame himself for this predicament.   Years later, he may now consciously see that his father was a harsh man who had his own problems, resulting in his critical attitudes.   Yet, unconsciously. my client still harbors the shame associated with his own sense of inadequacy.

Marriage is always, to some degree, a primary arena in which we hope as adults to heal our shame, by winning the approval of our spouse. Our logic is something like, "Since I failed to prove my value and worth to my primary caregivers in childhood, then I must succeed in adulthood by catching the brass ring of approval in my marriage." We also turn to our vocation, involvement in church or community, and any number of other arenas, in order to play a role that will secure approval.   Ideally, we must function flawlessly in any endeavor to reach that goal.

The problem we face, however, is that the brass ring seems to elude our grasp no matter how hard we try.   Other people, due to their own woundedness and sinfulness, refuse to acknowledge fully the sufficiency of our efforts.   Put simply, a person who does not like himself or herself is not going to give us the pleasure of their golden stamp of approval.   In addition, given the dynamics explained in the Mt. of Perfection model, we tend to over-compensate for shame by expecting too much of ourselves – virtual perfection.   Therefore, even if our spouse or boss is a reasonable person, we are setting ourselves up for failure if we assume that we should please them all the time in everything we do.

Such standards are also based on the false belief that we could be powerful enough to have total control over any other person's sentiments towards us. An example would be that I may think that I have pleased someone 99 days in a row, because he happens to greet me pleasantly each day at work; but perhaps it is only because I work at Wal-Mart, and the greeter at the main entrance is being paid to be nice. If, on the 100th day, the official greeter looks the other way when I come in, I may conclude that I have displeased him somehow, when in fact, he may have simply been distracted at that very second by something else happening in the store.

Remember, perfection is by definition all-or-nothing; we can't be half-perfect. The more shame we bear, the more we tend to expect perfection of ourselves in order to please others. Perfection always involves variables that God did not give us total control over – such as whether or not someone likes us or not. People choose how they will respond to us. If we are pleasant towards them, most likely they will be pleasant towards us, but that is their choice, not a response that we have created because we are so powerful. Conversely, while we may be unkind at times ourselves, people may respond by withdrawing from us, but that again is their choice.

My point is that *we **must** take responsibility for the unrealistic expectations that we create for ourselves in response to our shame*. The "*logic of shame*" tells us "we **have** to be perfect" in order to ever truly love and accept ourselves (and for God and other people to accept us as well). The first step in "freeing ourselves" from shame is to understand what unrealistic standards we have developed for ourselves in response to life events and situations that lead to shame-based beliefs. The hope is that we can understand that because such beliefs developed originally in the mind of a child, we no longer are compelled to live by them, and thus need not create perfect self-standards to compensate for them. Put simply, we can grasp the reality that we no longer *need* to be perfect, thus reducing the compulsion to be either a mountain-climber or a base-camper.

Let me encourage you to review the exercise that I suggested in the previous chapter: Observe yourself for the next week or two, in addition to thinking back over the course of your life. Check for any signs of intense over-reactions to situations. Usually, such situations involve emotional and behavioral responses of "***attacking***" (anger) or *"avoidance"* (fear). Then, ask yourself this very important question: *"What must I have expected of myself (not others!) in that situation, in order for me to react so strongly?"* Try to list a few major self-expectations of yourself, based on such observations, which border on perfectionism.

Let me give a personal example. Several years ago, I was out on a Sunday afternoon family drive with my wife and three daughters. We were exploring some of the seaside towns in Southeastern Massachusetts where we live, enjoying the beautiful scenery, when my wife asked a completely innocent question. She had recently taken over the responsibility of office manager for our growing counseling practice and "out of the blue" she inquired, "Did you remember to ask the Smiths for the $50 they owe us?" This was a simple question, requesting a simple "yes" or "no" answer. Instead of giving such a basic factual response, I acted very defensively, arguing that I cannot recall every detail of information that arises in my busy professional life. If I recall correctly, my response was in a question form such as, "Don't you know how many things I have to remember every day?" I soon realized I was over-reacting and blaming my wife for "causing" me to do so, since everything was going fine on our little trip until she asked the question.

Later that day, while wondering why I reacted so intensely, it occurred to me that apparently I expect myself to be so omniscient, so flawless, so superhuman, that I should never forget to do any task that my job requires. I, according to my own standards, not my wife's or my kids' or my coworkers, expect myself to be perfect!

Once we begin to accept this reality that *our real stresses in life come more from what we expect of ourselves than from what others expect of us*, the obvious question is how to become free from such self-demands. The next challenge is to replace such unrealistic expectations with those that are more "grace-based." The *"logic of grace"* is very simple but powerful: *Because Jesus Christ was and is perfect, I don't have to be"* (i.e., the New Testament Gospel in a nutshell). Hopefully, we can then grasp the profound truth that we no longer "have to be" perfect. No one really expects me to be perfect but myself. Once in a while, we do encounter a boss, church leader, friend, or spouse who does indeed seem to expect perfection of us.

However, *the real problem is not that others expect too much of me; it is that I expect myself to fulfill their expectations of me, no matter what they are.* We can spend a lifetime assuming that we must live up to whatever others expect of us; or we can see the truth that we have been making choices, albeit unconsciously, to live up to our own unrealistic self-demands. Once we realize this, then we can stand back from our over-reactions and try to define what perfectionist standards we apparently expect of ourselves, as I did after my explosion at my wife in the car that Sunday afternoon.

Having identified what our expectations must be, we can begin to choose new, more realistic ones. God has helped me over the years realize a very simple but profound truth: *I am a limited being*. As such, I am limited by time, energy, mental and physical power.   I cannot return calls saved on my voice mail while simultaneously counseling a client. I cannot recall every bit of data that I read or hear. I make mistakes. Moreover, most important, it is OK to be limited. Not to have limits would put me in the status of God Himself. I don't know about you, but I wouldn't want the responsibilities associated with that job!

While I say that, an underlying current of shame still propels me to be virtually perfect. I recall a supervisor I once had who, at the time, was a young, well-respected Christian psychiatrist. When I think of him, I recall the old "E.F. Hutton" stock broker TV commercials – "When E.F. Hutton speaks, everyone listens." My supervisor was a soft-spoken man who chose his words carefully. When he did speak in a meeting or case conference, our staff would listen with rapt attention, because he did have considerable wisdom and insight. He surprised me one day by sharing with me that he used to assume that everything he did say had to be quite wise and impressive, in keeping with what he assumed others expected of him as a young, Ivy League-trained psychiatrist. He had come to realize, however, that this standard was more of his own making than of others, and that he no longer *had to* be sure that every utterance he made was profound.

In essence, my supervisor discovered an important truth: He could now choose what he would expect of himself, regardless of what patients, coworkers, and others might have demanded of him. He was now *choosing* to be more gracious towards himself – to view himself as a well educated, wise, but still limited human being who does not always have all the answers and is capable of making mistakes. He was beginning to overcome the shame-based drive to be perfect, by setting more realistic and grace-based standards for himself.

While I am thinking about it, let me add that acknowledging and identifying our own perfectionist self-expectations is often difficult. Such standards have been woven into to our unconscious mind since childhood, so that they just seem to be a part of who we are. We need to put ourselves humbly at the mercy of God, asking him as limited creatures, to give us wisdom and insight in order to identify such standards. Also, owning up to perfectionism is hard for us to do, because we would much rather blame others for our stresses than accept the fact that our own reaction to shame is really the culprit. I chose to blame my wife for asking a legitimate question, rather than realize that her question simply triggered a reminder within myself that I had failed to be perfect in accordance with my own expectations. I needed to be more "grace-based" than "shamed-based" in my attitude towards myself, and in my approach towards her.

Dr. Larry Crabb summarizes the entire situation best by these words from his book, ***Finding God*** (1993): *"Grace frees me **from** needing to be better than I am and frees me **to** face what I'm really like without giving up."* (p.113)

For Reflection:

Try your hand at the following situations. See if you can identify unrealistic expectations each individual must have of him or herself in each scenario.

1. The man who screams angrily at his wife when she nicely asks him to roll down the window of the car and ask the policeman for directions.

2. The woman who wouldn't return to a Bible study, as a brand new Christian, after attending two times and having difficulty finding her place in Scripture and praying publicly.
3. The boy who has tried three sports and two musical instruments for only a few short months, states that he quickly has lost interest in each endeavor.
4. The highly successful businessman who feels mortified when his co-workers joyously relate the achievements of their teenagers, while his own son will not graduate with his class due to academic failure.

As stated earlier, many cognitive-oriented treatment approaches focus on changing the underlying negative beliefs in order to break this vicious cycle. In the realm of Christian self-help material, Robert McGee has written a fine book, *The Search for Significance* (1990), in which he cogently explains how erroneous beliefs about ourselves create negative emotional, relational, and spiritual consequences. He then clearly sets forth biblical doctrines which, when understood by the believer, can eradicate such false thinking; replacing our fear of failure, need for human approval, drive for perfectionism, and corresponding sense of shame with the peace and joy of justification, reconciliation, propitiation and regeneration. I love the way that McGee has laid out this model, including a two-page chart that consists of 4 columns, entitled, *False Beliefs, Consequences of False Beliefs, God's Specific Solution, and Results of God's Solution* (p.122-123).

At one point in my counseling ministry, I would show clients this grid and state that the ideal goal would be for them to move from column #1 to column #4 – from false beliefs and their corresponding consequences, to biblical beliefs about ourselves and their positive results. What freedom and relief we would then experience! What a strong sense of personal significance we would gain! I really like McGee's plan. In theory, it explains the roots of our pain and distress, and the pathway to ultimate healing.

While taking nothing away from Dr. McGee's fine book, my experience tells me that we do not progress neatly and cleanly across the chart. Our conscious logic quite easily grasps the truths of column

#4, but the emotional or "feeling" side of our nature is not so quickly convinced. We believe with our minds that we need not be perfect. As in the Mt. of Perfection model, we now know intellectually that *because Jesus Christ was and is perfect for us, we don't have to be.* However, as much as we try to remind ourselves of this truth, we are aware that deeper down in our soul, we cannot fully accept its reality.

If it were a matter of simple logic, I could assign all my clients fine books such as *Search for Significance* (and I still do). They would immediately grasp the truth of God's marvelous grace in such a way that their symptoms of anxiety and depression, along with feelings of low self-esteem, would immediately melt away. Evidently, this is not the case or my clients would not return as often as most of them do. Maybe they just need to read and re-read such material over and over again.

By the way, so as not to single out McGee's book, we have the same problem with Scripture itself. Lifelong Christians hear Biblical teaching over and over again – Sunday in and Sunday out. Yet, no matter how true Truth is, individual hearers respond differently to it, and no one receives, accepts and acts upon it completely and perfectly. We *know* we are sinners in need of forgiveness, we *know* that Christ has paid the penalty for our sin, we *know* that "there is now no condemnation for those who are in Christ Jesus" (Romans 8:1), and we *know* that we are accepted, loved, valued and counted as being righteous purely by God's grace.

Then why do we persist in *feeling* that we are inadequate, never quite good enough, and never totally able to rest in the reality of God's unmerited favor towards us?

Put another way, why do we not seem to truly love ourselves as God, through Scripture, claims to do? In his book, *Addiction and Grace*, author Gerald May appeals to the necessity of faith. He defines the "*risk of faith*" as learning to "*believe that what God says about me is more true than what I have learned to believe about myself.*" While agreeing wholeheartedly with this statement, I continue to observe within the experience of candid Christian believers, a lack of "heartfelt" fulfillment of such a risk.

Before attempting to answer the question of why there seems to be a perpetual discrepancy between what we know to be true with our "heads" and what we feel to be true in our "hearts, let me explain an important distinction. We confuse, and even fuse, two concepts that are actually quite different: One concept is that of "*value*," and the other is that of "*deservedness*."

By definition, value is "placed" upon an object, hence implying that the object in and of itself does not have inherent value. In counseling sessions, I use my wedding ring to exemplify this truth. My wedding ring as a physical object, a chunk of what we call "gold," has no "built in" worth or value. Its value is *attributed* to it from some external source(s). One source is myself – I give the ring value because of the many years of marriage that it represents. It has great symbolic or sentimental value to me personally. Another source would be those who determine what gold is worth at any given moment (my ring may or may not be worth anymore at a pawn shop than it was in 1977 when my wife and I purchased it). If I were to take the ring to Mars, and if indeed Martians did exist, they may view it has having no value whatsoever, either as a ring-shaped object, or as a gold object. On the other hand, they may decide that is has some other value altogether such as a replacement part for their spaceships. I have heard missionaries tell hilarious stories of how some of their personal objects have been used and valued (or "devalued") by native people in foreign countries.

Value, in other words, is relative. The value of an object always depends upon who is doing the valuing and what the object comes to mean to that person or persons. The value of a company's stock is an obvious example of this principle – it can change from minute to minute, day to day, month to month, etc., depending upon many variables outside of itself.

On the other hand, there is the concept of what I like to call "*deservedness*." This refers to the degree of reward that is earned, according to some scale that measures performance in respect to a specific dimension. This is what is called a "merit-based" system. A student may or may not deserve or "merit" a certain grade, based on his ability to perform according to a professor's standards. An employee may or may not deserve a raise, or for that matter, a paycheck, depending upon whether she has fulfilled specific job responsibilities.   An athlete may or may not deserve to play in the weekend game, depending upon whether or not he chose to attend daily practices that week.   There are many such situations in life, in which we deserve or do not deserve some sort of reward, depending upon our level or degree of performance.

The crucial distinction, however, between *value* and *deservedness* is this: value is conferred upon, or attributed to us. We do not earn it or fail to earn it.   It is totally unrelated to how flawed or flawless our performances may be in life activities.   It is strictly a quality that is given to us by God, through His free act of grace. **It is reflective of His character,** not our own.   However, because of who He is, and because He has loved and approved of us, we can then legitimately value ourselves.   In contrast, the notion of *deservedness* is reflective of *our behavior* or performance in life.   As we know from Scripture, we all deserve eternal perdition due to our innate sin nature (*All have sinned and fall short of the glory of God).* Because God is merciful, He restrains Himself from giving us what we actually do deserve. Due to his gracious nature, he freely gives us what we do not deserve, what we have not earned – i.e., value, worth, meaning, purpose, and the opportunity to enjoy intimate relationship with Him eternally.

Our problem is that *we confuse being valued with the compulsion to deserve God's favor.* We naturally assume that, as in virtually every other life situation, we are loved, admired, accepted and rewarded only if we work hard enough to deserve such accolades.   We thus try to earn something that is neither possible to earn (we could never be good enough), nor necessary to earn (the Perfection of Christ has fulfilled the requirements for us). How frustrated, yet patient God must be with us!

Imagine that as a parent, you try to give a fabulous gift to your child, yet your child refuses it because he or she would rather earn the right to have it.   It then would no longer be a gift if the child somehow could deserve it, and your joy as a parent would be greatly diminished.

Sometimes we do simply want to give a gift to express our love -- not to reward another's effort. I enjoy rewarding my children when they have performed a specific task appropriately. But, I love to "gift" them, especially with my love and acceptance of them, even when they do not necessarily perform activities to an optimal level. We often thwart God's gracious love and acceptance of us, as we assume that we must earn His favor. Phenomenally, God continues to love us even when we refuse His gift.

A prime Biblical example of this confusion between value and deservedness is Jesus' parable of the "*Workers in the Vineyard*" recorded in Matthew 20: 1-16. Jesus likens the Kingdom of Heaven to a landowner who hired workers at various intervals during the day, and when evening came, paid all the workers the same amount. The workers who began earlier in the day accused the landowner of being unfair. After all, should not they merit a higher wage for a longer day's work than those who worked as little as one hour?

According to a merit-based system, their complaint certainly holds water. However, in the logic of grace within God's Kingdom, members of the Kingdom are gifted by a God whose love flows freely, regardless of the deservedness of its recipients. As we know from many other sections of Scripture, all that is required by such recipients is to have faith in this God who loves them beyond the bounds of normal human reasoning. Once again, in response to the logic of shame, *the logic of grace frees us from "having" to be perfect in order to merit or deserve God's favor.*

Still, we have trouble receiving God's gracious acceptance of us. Many people have said to me that they know God has given them the free gift of his loving approval – His valuing of them. Yet, they cannot have that same attitude towards themselves. Picture God handing me a package representing His loving gift of acceptance and value, and I hold out my hands as a stop sign: "Thanks God. I know you love and accept me, but I cannot give myself the same gift – I don't deserve it....maybe if I work hard enough, someday I will deserve the right to love myself as you apparently do."

The logic of shame demands that we earn our acceptability, our significance. Exposing the shame for what it is – a false set of beliefs about ourselves, usually developed early in childhood, can lead to a new awareness that we *no longer "have" to be perfect in order to have value and worth*. Understanding the distinction between value and deservedness can help free us from a shame-based view of ourselves.

As implied earlier, however, there are various levels of "understanding," moving from the cognitive ("head knowledge") to a more complete awareness ("head and heart"). The term "comprehension" means to know something with the mind, whereas "apprehension" means to know something with the heart. How can this transition occur, so that we move beyond faulty logic to grasp the truth of God's grace, which can transform thoughts, feelings and behaviors? Why does it seem that even when people expose the sources of their shame (e.g. parental abuse or neglect), and then expose their unrealistic, perfectionistic expectations of themselves to compensate for their shame, they often still strive towards such expectations? When I finally learn that I no longer need to be perfect, then why do I observe myself continuing to strive in that direction, assuming the stance of either a *mountain-climber* or a *base-camper*?

One answer to this dilemma may be that the logic of shame is often buried in relatively deep levels of consciousness. This can be true because it develops in some of us at such an early age that it predates self-awareness and even the development of language. In other words, its genesis occurs even before a child is able to consciously say to herself that she is shameful or worthless. Recall the example from Chapter 1 about the 18-month-old girl who assumed that she should be able to diffuse the violence that would erupt between her parents. Years later, she would never remember the scene in my office when she attempted to draw attention to herself, and divert her parents' focus from their own conflict. Yet, this memory and its meaning would be etched in her psyche forever, including the shame-based assumption that she is a failure because she could not perform a task that was beyond her God-given capabilities. This "core" belief that she is shameful, would naturally persist, partly because its roots were unconscious.

Occasionally, an adult can look back and now realize that it was not her fault that her parents divorced; and perhaps this realization can lead to a release from unrealistic expectations and correlated shame. Even then, she can work hard to consciously convince herself that her current husband's failure to love her is not an indictment on her value and worth. However, the degree of "apprehension" of this truth is usually rather limited. So, what if the situations, events, and relationships that marked the origin of shame-based logic are buried in the annals of subconscious memories? How then could such a person ever truly grasp the truth of God's gracious acceptance when the unconscious roots of shame continue to powerfully drive the way one interprets and responds (feelings and behaviors) to life events?

Throughout the history of modern psychiatry and psychology there has been an ongoing tension between theories that emphasize the biological and neurochemical roots of thought processes and emotions, and on the other hand, theories that focus on non-physical ideas or "constructs." Before Sigmund Freud, medical doctors attempted to understand how "psychological illnesses" were linked to specific areas of the physical brain. Freud himself, though medically trained, left the realm of direct physical inquiry and developed theoretical ideas about how thoughts, feelings and behaviors originate. The "Id, Ego, and Superego" are terms that have found their way into the common English language, yet no one has ever proven their existence in the physical structures of the brain.

The entire notion of consciousness, and various levels of conscious awareness, is still being debated today. What does it mean to be conscious? Is it purely a physical and biological phenomena, or does it some how transcend the "matter" of the brain? Even the concept of the human "mind" becomes very complex when we attempt to dissect it into either physical or non-physical phenomena. What is the difference, if any, between what we call the "mind" and what we call the physical "brain?"

Likewise, throughout the history of the Christian church, attempts have been made to grasp the relationship between body and soul ("psyche") or even body, soul, and "spirit." Many questions arise in this debate over what components comprise a human being, and most are beyond the scope of this book. However, it is important to realize that thoughts and emotions, such as those associated with the logic of shame, are not simply non-material entities floating somewhere in our head or "hearts," but that every idea and feeling does represent some physiological process in the brain. Unlike the days of Freud in the early 20th century, we do have technology today that can allow us to observe and monitor physiological and chemical changes in the brain as they correspond to thinking processes and feeling states. Even now, though, no one has claimed to "see" an Id or an Ego in the physical brain, let alone a soul or spirit, and I doubt that anyone ever will.

It is sufficient to conclude that we are holistic beings whose spiritual natures intermingle with our physical brains and bodies. Psychologist David Benner suggests in his book, *Care of Souls* (1998) that we can view ourselves as "somotopsychospiritual" beings (p.51). He defines the "soul" as the place where the spirit and psyche meet. What we call psychological processes – thinking, feeling, willing, desiring, etc. – combine with our human spirit, which in turn can commune with God's Spirit within us. This "soul" is also embodied in our physical body ("soma" in Greek).

Every therapist like my self who has been in the field for a while, has recognized that attempting to replace one set of false cognitive beliefs with a more positive and Biblically correct set is easier said than done. Changing our thoughts alone does not usually seem to have a powerful impact upon the other aspects of our personhood. Unfortunately, stress-induced emotional and physical symptoms tend to persist even after profound cognitive insight is achieved.

Some relatively recent innovations in the fields of psychology and neurology would suggest why this might be. There is some evidence to suggest that thoughts and emotions are stored in separate sections of the brain. In very general terms, the left hemisphere appears to be where cognitive activity occurs and the right hemisphere where emotional processes take place. Several years ago, one of my own colleagues introduced me to a novel counseling tool called "Eye Movement Desensitization and Reprocessing" (EMDR), which I first dismissed as a passing fad and probably a product of the New Age movement. What sparked my interest, however, was the fact that clients who struggled for years with their own logic of shame and corresponding emotional, relational and spiritual dysfunction, were now beginning to "feel" God's grace, in addition to simply knowing about it with their minds.

I have been using this tool consistently now for several years with significant results. For years, I had helped people cope with the wounds of their past, holding their anxieties and depressions at bay. Some of these same clients began to be truly healed from the wounds of their past, believing with their heart, mind and even physical bodies that regardless of how others' sin may have affected them, and regardless of how their own sin had offended others, they were indeed valuable, worthwhile sons and daughters of a just and loving God. As one of my own clients put it, EMDR helped him to not only *comprehend* that God loved him, but to *apprehend* the fact as well. As we mentioned earlier, the dictionary defines "comprehension" as knowing something with one's mind, whereas to "apprehend" means to know something with one's heart.

I do not intend here to glorify this particular counseling tool, but to highlight it as one means of working with the complex mind-body-soul interaction. While researchers continue to speculate as to why and how it works, EMDR uses the stimulation of both hemispheres of the brain as a means of releasing what appears to be a God-given internal capacity to heal psychological wounds. According to this model, the logic of shame is stored in one area of the physical brain, whereas the emotions and physical feeling states associated with it are locked in other sections. EMDR helps integrate these various components so that the sense of shame dissolves in the thinking, emotions and physical being of the client. Readers are invited to explore more about this powerful counseling tool on their own (www.emdr.com).

Over the course of writing this book, I have become aware of other techniques, similar to EMDR, which go beyond traditional "talk therapy" and address the way in which thoughts and feelings are stored in the physical body. I am open to exploring the validity of such approaches to healing, believing that God's "common grace", as in the medical sciences, allows believers and unbelievers alike to make wonderful discoveries. Yet, I also prayerfully investigate such new techniques, asking for God's wisdom to recognize underlying philosophies that may contradict the truths of Scripture.

Our current purpose is only to remind us that there appears to be more to fully grasping the reality of God's truth with our entire being than just acknowledging it with our thinking capacities. It is for this reason that we often have difficulty "absorbing" God's grace. As we

Christians are fond of saying, "We live in a fallen world." Since this is true, it should not be hard to imagine that sin has negatively affected not just our minds and spirits, but our bodies as well. Birth defects are one obvious example of the effects of living in a fallen world. If they can occur, then why cannot our physical brains (bone, blood, chemicals, electric impulses, etc.) also be corrupted by sin? We might then be wise to consider the influence of "infected matter" and not just "distorted thinking" when we attempt to gain freedom from the logic of shame. Modern "psychotropic" medicines may also then play a role in a balanced, Biblically-based approach to healing and "growth in grace."

Let's return once more to our discussion about our shame-based drive towards perfection. Rabbi Harold Kushner is probably best known for his book, *When Bad Things Happen to Good People* (1981). One of my clients presented me with a lesser-known work by the same author, entitled, *How Good Do I Have to Be?* (1996) Rabbi Kushner's response to his own question translates into, "As good as you can be." He suggests a form of "unconditional acceptance" which does not quite correspond with what we are talking about here. Rabbi Kushner acknowledges that God is perfect, but a benevolent God would never expect imperfect creatures to become perfect like Himself. Thus, it is only reasonable to assume that God simply expects us to try our best. When we sin, we should confess, "dust ourselves off," and try to do better next time.

With all due respect to Rabbi Kushner, I think he misses a very fundamental truth in the Hebrew Scriptures, or what Christians call the Old Testament: God, being perfectly holy, cannot allow any thing or person into his presence that also is not holy. The specific details of God's law concerning worship – the layout of the Tabernacle and later the Temple, the numerous rules concerning consecration of priests and sacrifices, etc. – all point to this reality. No one could even come into the "Holy of Holies," except the High Priest, once a year, after much ceremonial cleansing. In addition, when Moses and others experienced God's presence in a direct manner, the ground or the mountain was always "holy." When God instructed no one to touch the Ark of the Covenant directly, he meant what he said, as was displayed by the death of Uzzah, who tried to steady it. God did not say, "I know your intentions were basically good, so I will give you another chance. . ." No, the penalty for disobeying a perfectly Holy God was immediate death. Earlier, the Ark had been captured by the Philistines. After they were plagued by God, they returned it to Israel, and the first stop on the journey was the village of Beth Shemesh. 1 Samuel Chapter 6 tells us that, *"God struck down some of the men of Beth Shemesh, putting seventy of them to death because they had looked into the ark of the Lord."* The people of the village mourned and asked, *"Who can stand in the presence of the Lord, this Holy God?"*

The truth from the Old Covenant is that a Perfect God *does* indeed require perfection of us. Without the Good News of the New Covenant, this is a terrifying thought. Once again, we are left with the two main options of climbing the mountain of perfection as frantically as possible, or we give up all together and don't even try. But thanks be to God for his "unspeakable gift!" **The Good News of the New Covenant is that Jesus fulfilled God's requirement of perfection for us.** The overarching story of Scripture centers on an omnipotent Creator who amazingly desires to enter into relationship with his creatures. However, because he cannot compromise His own Being, he cannot have an intimate relationship with fallen, sinful creatures. Jesus Christ solves the problem by bridging the gap between God's holiness and our own imperfection (*"No man comes to the father but through me"* – *John 14:6*).

We also know from our Old Testament that approval in God's eyes did not come from fulfilling the demands of the complex laws. It was one's faith in the coming Messiah who would be that perfect mediator between God and man that enabled one to be "clothed" with Christ (Galatians 3:27) as Paul terms it. Abraham "believed" and it was "credited to him as righteousness" (Genesis 15:6, Romans 4:3). What exactly did he believe in? He believed that God would fulfill his covenant surely; but specifically that such fulfillment would come through his "seed" meaning Christ Himself (Galatians 3:16).

"Being clothed" with Christ's righteousness means that we ourselves do not actually become perfectly pure. Instead, God now views us and treats us as if we are pure, because He sees the purity of His Son covering our impurity.

Returning to our two "travelers" in the *Introduction* to this book, let's see what would happen if Alice and Ben could learn that they no longer "had" to be perfect; if they realized that they could be freed from the shameful belief the world imparts that one must perform perfectly to be fully acceptable.

First, you recall Alice – the "Type A" driven young woman ("*mountain-climber*") who always succeeded in every endeavor, from childhood through adolescence (high school and college) and into the stage of marriage and child rearing. As a super-diligent Christian, Alice believed she must perform flawlessly until one day the stress on her mind and body led to a "melt-down." With the help of the Holy Spirit's enlightenment, and perhaps through the aide of wise human counsel, Alice could learn that she does not have to be perfect in order to have value and identity. She could gain insight into the reality that her shame-based belief of not being ok "just as she is" derives from at least two major sources. First, there was the environment around her as a child -- she was born as the oldest in a large family with very busy parents.

The second source was her own interpretation of the situation, which was that her place or role in the family involved being very responsible as the first born, one upon whom parents and siblings depended greatly. As a young girl, Alice naturally assumed that this role gave her purpose, meaning, identity and significance as a human being. This "core belief" then led to the basic assumption that she must maintain a pattern of flawlessly completing responsibilities throughout her entire life. Without such performance and corresponding approval, there was no Alice. For Alice, the *logic of shame* could be summarized as, "Thou shalt not have limitations." Eventually, her mind and body told her that she did indeed have limitations of time, energy, resources, know-how, etc.

However, Alice can now see as an adult looking back, that she was not born with an innate sense of shame or inadequacy. This only developed as she interacted with an imperfect and shame-filled world. Such insights would be the first steps towards "growing in grace." Then, realizing that since God, through Christ, does not require perfection of her, she could be more accepting of her own limitations.

Our second "life-traveler" was young Ben, who in contrast to Alice developed a pattern of avoiding tasks and responsibilities ("*base-camper*"), unless he believed he could really excel (as in playing the drums). As the youngest of three brothers in a high achieving family, Ben's logic of shame told him that he also was not "ok" just as he was – he would have to achieve, especially academically and athletically, to the very high degree that his father and brothers had done. He eventually chose self-sabotage in those two areas, as a means of avoiding the even greater sense of shame that he presumed would result if he tried his very best and then fell short of perfection.

With proper direction, Ben also could become free from the shame-based belief that he must perform flawlessly to be an acceptable, relevant human being. A caring youth pastor, older mentor and/or a skilled counselor could help Ben realize that he is unique in his interests and abilities, and that because God created him that way, he need not worry about trying to be someone he wasn't.

Rather than sabotaging himself academically, for example, Ben could learn that he is free to try his very best, which may or may not result in formal grades that compare with those of his brother. *Grace means that he is free to explore his own thoughts, wishes, desires, and goals, instead of automatically assuming that he must conform to others' ideas of who he should be and what he should do.* He could be freed to decide for himself if he wants to work hard in certain subjects because he actually enjoys them – and do the same with a sport. People like Ben who are "avoiders" never give themselves the chance to decide whether they really do have a personal desire to engage in activities and fulfill responsibilities that they perceive others to be forcing upon them.

I have made this point repeatedly to adolescents who are in a rebellious mode. When they perceive (and often I believe there is some accuracy to their perceptions) that parents and others are manipulating them towards certain behaviors or the acceptance of certain belief systems, they run the other direction. "*If my parents are forcing Christianity down my throat, I'll become a pagan, or I'll check out Buddhism, just to prove that I am free.*" Yet, whenever we react to something, we are never really free from it; we have only gone to the other extreme, thinking that either that or total compliance are the only options.

I encourage such young people to *"**respond**"* rather than *"**react**."* I am reacting if, when parents seem to demand all A's, I chose to get F's just to prove that they cannot control me. I am responding to others' expectations if I stand back for a minute, and determine for myself what I really want to do, or how I want to live my life. I may just chose to strive for all A's, if I truly feel fulfilled in such a pursuit, whether others want me to or not.

There is nothing wrong with striving for excellence (not perfection) in any area of life, if we indeed feel free to pursue particular goals or levels of performance. However, we are never able to experience such freedom if we demand that high levels of performance are required in order to establish our self-worth.

Grace frees the Alices of the world to try their best in a limited number of pursuits as busy mothers, wives, church workers, etc. It frees them to decide what activities they genuinely want to be involved in, and how much time and effort they chooses to exert. It no longer matters what others think or desire for them, and most importantly, they no longer demand flawless perfection from themselves.

Grace frees the Bens of the world to chose for themselves what goals are important, and to "give it their best shot" without worrying about falling short of an ideal level of achievement. Are you more like Alice or Ben in your approach to the tasks of life? Perhaps you combine both styles in your own unique way. Ask the Holy Spirit to reveal to you the sources of your shame and the manner(s) in which you attempt to either cover over and/or compensate for it. Then seek, with God's help, to bask in the light of the reality that you do not have to prove your value and worth to Him, others or yourself.

Chapter 6:

Freedom from Ourselves: *Confessing our Pride*

While the logic of shame declares that we ***must*** be perfect in order to win the approval of others, ourselves, and God, the logic of pride goes one step further and asserts, "I ***want*** to be perfect." In the previous chapter, I mentioned a colleague of mine who expressed great relief, when as an austere mental health professional, he realized that not everything he said *had* to be perfectly profound. The reason his statement made such an impact upon me was that I was somewhat like him. Not yet having achieved my highest academic degree, I assumed that especially when I did have those letters after my name, I would also be required to give perfectly wise advice in any situation that I encountered. Therefore, hearing my friend, who had already been in the field for several years, make such a statement was strongly encouraging to me. I shared in his newfound freedom, at least for a while.

As is true of most new insights, we view the world in a new light; but then assume that this one novel perspective on life will immediately and totally change everything for us. It is much like the new convert to Christianity who indeed has begun to grasp a new and revolutionary set of truths and for several months remains on a spiritual high. Eventually, she begins to notice with the passage of time that she has not changed all that much, nor necessarily, has life itself. This usually leads to at least confusion, if not disillusionment.

In my case, I observed that something still propelled me towards my own unique mountain peaks of perfection. Even though I now realized that I did not "have" to be perfect, I continued to strive for flawlessness anyway. Somehow, I'm sure through the enlightenment of the Holy Spirit, I came to realize that in addition to shame, I struggled with "old fashioned" human **pride** – the desire recorded in Genesis when the first two humans wanted to be like God. If they were to eat from the tree of forbidden fruit, then they assumed that they could gain knowledge that would supplant the need for God, since they would know what He knew (the "tree of the knowledge of good and evil"). While the logic of shame says, "I *must* be perfect" in order to compensate for my unworthiness, the logic of pride states, "I *want* to make myself perfect, on my own….to make myself acceptable" (self-righteousness and also self-sufficient).

As mentioned in Chapter 5, one reason that grace is difficult to grasp completely is that the logic of shame, which thwarts grace, may be buried in the unconscious mind, and perhaps even to some degree, in the physical matter of our brains. However, I am going to suggest that a greater obstacle to "growing in grace" is our pride. We do not really want to receive a free gift; we would rather believe that we had done something to deserve it. This is why some folks actually repel gifts.

I recall counseling a teenage girl, who had left her own home due to strife with her parents, and was taken in by a friend's family. I do not remember the nature of the difficulties in her family life, but the fact is that her logic of shame was rather intense. Whatever went wrong with her parents, she ultimately blamed herself for it, ("I apparently don't deserve my parents' love as do other kids whose parents treat them appropriately"). When she came to live with her friend's family, she was treated not only with dignity and respect, but also as someone uniquely valuable. I listened as she recounted how this new family had arranged a surprise birthday party for her. When I expressed joy on her behalf, she surprised me with the opposite response. Instead of welcoming this free gift of love, she ran and hid in the garage.

Many times during my career, I have counseled people (usually women, but some men as well) who ask me how it could be that they have gone from one failed relationship to another. One particular young woman had been married three times to three abusive husbands. As the third relationship was crumbling, she asked me one day, "*Why didn't I say 'yes' to the man who was the first to ask me to marry him – a young man who treated me with tenderness and respect, and now is a happily married minister? Instead, I sabotaged the relationship, and eventually chose to marry these other men.*"

There are probably numerous ways in which professional therapists may attempt to answer this question, but here is my own "take" on the situation: When I have experienced shame, my innate pride jumps into action. The fact that I think so poorly of myself now gives me an enticing situation – I *desire* to work hard enough to prove that I am worthy of others' approval. To accomplish this, I need an appropriate challenge. Remember, the depth of my shame is inversely related to the height of my mountain peaks. The worse I think and feel about myself, the higher I now *want* to climb in order to show that *I,* and I alone, can do what it takes to be worthy. That's why a free gift actually defeats my purpose. If something is free, I don't have to earn it; if I don't have to earn it, then my prideful self will never have the opportunity to prove that I actually can deserve the gift.

The young teenager who fled the birthday party not only struggled with shame from parental rejection, but her pride created further problems by demanding that she compensate for her own shame. When her host family gave her the grace of a surprise party, she recoiled, not only because she "didn't deserve it," but also because she *wanted* to deserve it. Likewise, the young divorcee first sabotaged a relationship in which her suitor loved her as she was. Because she could not accept who she thought she was (filled with shame), she fled that relationship, and then built higher "relational mountains." She did so by unconsciously allowing herself to be attracted to men whose approval was quite conditional. As long as she could conform to their wishes and desires, she had a significant challenge. The logic of pride says, *"The more it takes for me to win someone's approval, the more opportunity I have to prove that I can make myself good enough. If someone's love and acceptance is unconditional, then my pride has no opportunity to flourish."*

I like to phrase the situation this way: Our pride "piggy-backs" on our shame. I have already mentioned the observation that we are not so much victimized by our pasts, as we are by our responses to the past. According to the *Mountain of Perfection Model*, I now struggle more with my prideful attempts to heal my own shame, than with the original shame itself. Larry Crabb has defined "sin" in a variety of helpful ways, one of which involves our attempts to heal our woundedness independently from God (cf. *Finding God,* chapter 8). Like Adam and Eve, we want to run the show, even in terms of achieving our own worthiness, which God has already attributed to us. In a related manner, Dr. Crabb also would define sin as a "failure to trust in God's ultimate goodness." Pride says to God, "I neither trust You as the sole source of my value, meaning and purpose, nor do I need You to find my own way in life."

A woman who was intensely abused as a child, now attempts, especially as a Christian mother, to protect her children, perfectly of course, from any and all forms of evil. One loving motive would certainly be that she does not want her kids to ever experience what she did. However, being a prideful being like the rest of us, she also hopes to prove that she is capable of achieving this impossible goal on her own. Consciously she prays to God, serves in the church, reads her Bible, etc. However, unconsciously, she is driven by shame and pride to compensate for her horrible sense of self – *"Look how wonderful I would be if I could ever achieve such an impossible goal! In fact, other women I know come from loving Christian homes and obviously learned to love themselves more naturally. But, the fact that I have a much more intense sense of shame now gives me the chance to climb higher mountains of perfection than they need to."*

Let me reiterate, that just as the logic of shame is often unconscious, I think that we are even better at repressing, if not denying altogether, our pride. Especially when the shame is conscious, it is difficult to be aware of pride. How can we accuse a person, who blatantly hates herself, of having pride? Well, here is why: after events and situations occur to create shame in our psyches, pride sets out actually to recreate more shame. Take the woman who struggled with an inability to please three abusive husbands. Regardless of her original sources of shame, she set out on the prideful quest to prove that she was worthy, and thus unconsciously sought relationships that would test her ability to earn approval to compensate for the shame. However, because her mountain peaks represented impossible tasks (i.e., to win the love of men who, due to their own shame and pride, did not love themselves in a godly manner), she was only setting herself up for perceived failure. Each time a marriage failed, she would consciously blame the husband, but on some level of awareness, she assumed that the problem lay with her unworthiness. Each time she failed to win approval, she believed even more strongly that she was the ultimate problem.

Another woman once told me about the affair her husband recently had. Her pastor told her clearly that she was not at fault and that she even had Biblical grounds for divorce, if she so chose. While feeling justifiably hurt, she remarked to me, *"I can't help wondering what was wrong with me that he found another woman more attractive."*

You see, when pride follows shame, a vicious cycle ensues. It is frankly difficult for me to articulate the exact relationship between shame and pride. I am not entirely sure which comes first in our experience, or that it necessarily matters. It does seem reasonable to assume from the biblical doctrine of original sin that we come into this world as prideful beings. The infant or young child is obviously not aware of his innate self-centeredness, but the parent certainly notices this aspect of a child's nature at least by toddler hood. If we conceptualize the time-line of a person's life, then beginning at birth we are prideful, self-centered beings.

As time rolls on, sooner or later we experience shame. Of course, even if we never felt shame, we would still be sinners. Thus, when shame does occur, it is inevitable that we would respond to it in some sinful, self-centered manner. This does, in fact, suggest that of the two conditions, shame and pride, the latter is the more fundamental. Then the vicious cycle is off and running: *By responding to my shame through prideful attempts to heal my shame perfectly, I only create further shame as I perceive that I have failed to achieve perfection. I am then tempted to try even harder to compensate for my renewed sense of shame by achieving even greater heights of perfection.*

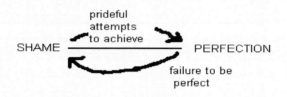

The challenge, therefore, is to find freedom from not only shame, but pride as well. People who have been victimized (and we all have to one degree or another), often hold themselves accountable for what they in reality are not responsible for. Yet, they fail to accept responsibility for what they should be held accountable. Put another way, they blame themselves for something that was not their fault (the events and situations that developed a sense of shame). As we have already discussed, this is a normal response in childhood to assume too much responsibility for situations beyond one's control, such as an adult choosing to abuse a child. However, as that child matures, he naturally fails to recognize that and assumes responsibility for his prideful attempts to compensate for shame. Whatever these specific attempts entail, they always involve the desire to be perfect.

An increased awareness of God's grace allows us to understand that we do not need to blame and shame ourselves for how others have wounded us. Much of modern psychotherapy, both Christian and secular, aims at having the victim place blame where it is due – upon the perpetrator. Some call this "externalizing the shame," pushing outward from ourselves to the world around us from which it came. **However, an even more crucial goal of Christ-centered counseling must be to recognize our prideful drive to heal ourselves from shame through perfectionism**. Only by God's grace do we even become aware of such pride; and only through the work of grace in our hearts and minds do we confess, repent, and begin upon the path of freedom from such pride.

Let us be very clear about one crucial point: ***We cannot free ourselves from our own pride***. To assume that we could is prideful in it self. Through what the Old Testament calls "severe mercy," God's Spirit gradually enlightens us as to the presence of pride in our hearts, and the subtle forms of its expression. That mercy is "severe," because we often need to come to a point of "brokenness" through what can be painful experiences. It is painful to continue trying to achieve flawlessness and repeatedly fail, then to "beat ourselves up" for failing, only to try harder again. We wear ourselves out and sooner or later crash, which is never fun. As Christians going through this process, we of course, wonder where our Loving Father is when we need him. Just as in the parable, He is waiting patiently for his prodigal son or daughter to get tired of slopping around with the swine and return home.

A Healthy Response to Pride: Godly Sorrow

There are actually two forms of "***brokenness***" that are sometimes confused by the Christian community. One is the experience of breaking down due to the vicious cycle mentioned above. The *mountain climber* finally crashes, or the *base-camper* eventually admits that he hates the fact that he has never achieved any worthwhile goal, but then goes on to hate himself. When perceived failure leads to increased shame, then an ungodly form of brokenness occurs, which either fuels a desperate need for help, or a further withdrawal from the world. The Apostle Paul refers to this as "*worldly sorrow*" in 2 Corinthians 7:10, which he says, "brings death." It may not immediately lead to physical death, but it does kill the spirit of hope within a person. In contrast, Paul speaks in the same verse of a "*godly sorrow*" which "*brings repentance that leads to salvation and leaves no regret,…*" Godly sorrow leads to confession and repentance. This should indeed be our response when, by His Grace, God's Spirit within us convicts us of our prideful attempts to heal our own woundedness.

Two prominent New Testament characters help illustrate how shame and pride inter-relate: **Judas Iscariot** and the **Apostle Peter.** They had at least five things in common:

1) Both were **called and anointed by Jesus**: *"Jesus went up on a mountainside and called to him those he wanted, and they came to him. He appointed 12 designating them apostles – that they might be with him and that he might send them out to preach and to have authority to drive out demons."* (Mark 3:13-15) Also, in Matthew 10, Jesus gave them the power "to heal every disease and sickness."

2) Both **lived with Jesus:** He had no place to lay his head, thus they shared with him a rugged life-style (ideal for "male-bonding"). Both Peter and Judas would have been eyewitnesses of Jesus' miracles; they ate and fellowshipped with him; they listened to his teachings, such as the Sermon on the Mount and all of his parables (and were privileged to have Jesus explain them). In short, they experienced the highs and lows of Jesus' ministry from a first-hand vantage point – right there with Him. Peter was especially privileged to be able to walk on water with Jesus' help (Matthew 14) and to be present along with James and John at the Transfiguration. Peter was also the one to whom Jesus declared, *"On this rock I will build my church."* Peter actually held the position of leadership in the circle of the Twelve. He is mentioned first in the four lists of the twelve disciples in the New Testament. In the Gospels, he is the most frequently mentioned of the Twelve. Even more amazing, then, that he would later betray Jesus, having had such an intimate relationship with Him.

3) *Jesus predicted ahead of time that Peter & Judas each would betray him:* At the Last Supper, after Jesus washed the disciples' feet, Jesus stated that the one who would betray him *"is the one to whom I will give this piece of bread I have dipped in the dish"* (John 13). That one, of course was Judas. Also at the same supper, Jesus said to the group, *"This very night you will all fall away on account of me."* Peter then pledged his allegiance – *"Even if all fall away on account of you, I will never...even if I have to die with you, I will never disown you!"* Jesus then responded with his famous prediction that before the *"cock crows three times,"* Peter would indeed disown his Lord.

4) *Both Judas and Peter willingly and deliberately betrayed Jesus:* In spite of all they had both experienced being with

Jesus for 3 years, and in spite of His prediction that they would fail Him, they did so anyway. Peter had even made the well-known "confession" in Matthew 16: *"You are the Christ, the Son of the Living God."* Judas sold Jesus for 30 pieces of silver, handing him over to the Jewish authorities. Peter denied Jesus not once, but three times, as Jesus was going through a series of trials. He literally disassociated himself from the One to whom he had been so close and Who loved him so dearly.

5) ***Having betrayed Christ, both would have known, having been with Christ, His gracious and forgiving nature:*** We can assume, for example, that the disciples were all right there when the Pharisees and the teachers of the law brought to Jesus the woman caught in adultery (John 8). When the brief encounter was over, Jesus simply forgave the woman, saying, *"Then neither do I condemn you…Go now and leave your life of sin"* (vs. 11). The most profound example of Jesus' gracious and forgiving nature was His willingness to serve his disciples, not only washing their feet, but also willing to die on their behalf.

While Judas and Peter were similar in these five ways, how were they different from one another? Once Judas had realized what he had done – betrayed the Son of Man, handing Him over for crucifixion – he killed himself. One gospel says that he did so by hanging, and another by throwing himself headlong into a field he had bought. Peter, on the other hand, received God's forgiveness and continued to fulfill his role as one of the most prominent Apostles after Jesus' ascension. Why, then, was Peter able to receive Jesus' forgiveness and in turn, forgive himself, and why was Judas not able to do so?

I believe that both of these disciples assumed that they had crossed the "big line" – they had gone too far, and were beyond forgiveness (as any one of us may believe at some point in our lives). It was a hopeless situation in their minds and hearts. There was absolutely nothing they could do to undo or make up for what had been done. While it is always risky to "read between the lines" of Scripture, let me offer some ideas that I think are at least strongly implied in the biblical accounts of these events. Judas assumed that it was his job to atone, or make up for, what he had done; yet he knew down deep that he could never really do so. His final sin was not his betrayal per se, but his **prideful assumption** that he could and should pay back the debt that he now owed Jesus.

Like the Pharisees, Judas desired self-righteousness, rather than accepting Christ's righteousness (*"I can, and want to, make myself better and worthy of God's approval "*). Yet realizing that he could never be good enough to compensate for the horrible deed he had just committed, he put himself in a proverbial "Catch-22". Or to put it more bluntly, he was "damned if he did try (he knew he would fail), but also "damned if he didn't try." Thus, he gave himself no way out. To take it one step further, perhaps Judas even postulated that taking his own life would be sufficient atonement, thus satisfying the debt of guilt that he owed – *"If I suffer enough, maybe that will convince Jesus that I still love him and he will forgive me."* I have known people who themselves have taken very drastic measures, even severe forms of self-harm, to convince others of their devotion.

Judas suffered not only from intense guilt, (*"I have done something terribly wrong"*), but his prideful belief that he should be able to atone for his guilt only created a sense of intense personal shame ("*I am worthless because I cannot right this wrong, but I really wish I could do so by my own efforts"*). Here is where shame and pride converge, creating a new layer of confusion and self-denigration over the original layer of legitimate guilt. To feel convicted of wrongdoing is unpleasant, if not gut-wrenching at times, but to assume that I should be able to make myself worthy, and to desire to do so, only creates an impossible goal that I am doomed to fall short of, declaring myself a shameful failure. At this point in Judas' mind, suicide was the logical extension either of such shame-based self-hatred, or as just stated, maybe it represented a last-ditch prideful effort to do *something* to regain his acceptable status before the Messiah.

Let's now turn to Peter: We read in John 21 that after fishing in vain all night, the disciples were aided by Jesus in landing an entire "boatload" of fish. Then he prepared a breakfast for the weary fishermen (once again, Jesus *serves them*). Finally, he declares his forgiveness to Peter who had betrayed him three times, by giving him the opportunity to pledge his love and allegiance to Jesus three times. As Jesus had earlier predicted, Church tradition does state that Peter was eventually martyred, but that is much different from taking his own life. Instead, he served Christ for the remainder of his earthly life by going on to "feed Jesus' sheep" (i.e., to minister to and serve others in the name of Christ).

Peter would not have been able to move on successfully with his life had he not received Jesus' gracious gift of forgiveness. The picture I have in my mind is of Jesus handing us a beautifully wrapped package (mostly likely gold in color!) that represents his free gift of grace – his forgiveness for our sins and his continued love for us in spite of our sinful condition. Like any other gift, we then must decide what we will do with it – we can either reach out and take it with our own hands, open it up and partake of its splendor, or we can refuse the gift, turn and walk away. It is not possible for the giver to force the potential recipient to take the gift, because if the recipient only receives it under pressure, then it really is no longer a free gift.

Peter did accept Jesus' gift of forgiveness, and then turned around and applied the gift to himself. How could he have done that? Like Judas, he realized that his sin was so profound that he could never have atoned for it. However, unlike Judas, Peter did not despair. He realized that Christ had already atoned for his sin. Because Christ had suffered the penalty for sin, he did not have to. Because *Christ was righteous for* Peter, Peter did not have to become perfectly pure by his own efforts. While Judas's ultimate sin was pride, Peter instead humbly admitted both his sin and his limitations as a human being – his inability to pay Jesus back for his sin.

With such humility, Peter did not pridefully attempt to "earn his own salvation," which is an impossible task surpassing human limitations. Thus, he did not have to experience the shame of not being someone he could never be in the first place – a flawless being. *Peter knew that he needed forgiveness for what he had done; but not for who he was – a limited creature dependent upon a limitless Creator.*

Shame, as we have defined it, arises from the assumption that we could and should be better than we are, only to experience failure in achieving such a goal, resulting in self-hatred. In contrast, a legitimate and healthy sense of guilt (*godly sorrow*) allows us to acknowledge our sinful behavior and our sinful condition in general, but without self-loathing. God never loathes his creatures, but we often loath one another, and often times our own selves, as when people say such things as, "*I know God forgives me, but I just cannot forgive myself.*" Such an attitude reflects this self-loathing that flows naturally from the prideful assumption that we can and should be able to make ourselves fully acceptable to God. God, however, understands our inability to overcome our own sinful nature, and loves us anyway, as he did in Peter's case.

Another angle here involves the main point of focus for Peter and Judas. The latter man focused on himself - his sin, his guilt, his estrangement from Christ, his desire to win back Christ's approval by his own efforts. **In contrast, Peter focused more on who Christ was, and what Christ had already done for him. His eyes were looking outward and forward towards the Source of pure righteousness, while Judas' prideful eyes could only focus on his own sorry state.**

The relationship between shame and pride is perhaps more complex than I personally can conceive. Yet, as stated earlier, it does appear that pride can "piggy back" on top of shame, which means that once shame has settled into a person's psyche ("*I am worthless*"), then pride seizes the opportunity by asserting that one could, and actually desires to, heal one's own shame. A person could even compare her perceived depth of shame with that of another: "*She comes from a loving family, whereas I came from a very abusive one. The depth and intensity of my shame is therefore much greater than hers is. So, if I could achieve some height of perfection, then I would have had to work a lot harder than she would – thus making me better or more worthy of approval.*"

Now, watch what happens next: Having allowed her pride to create an unachievable goal (perfection), then she has set herself up for more shame. She will only sense failure, sooner or later, as she realizes that she cannot achieve flawlessness in certain or all areas of life, and then comes the horrible sense of total (all-or-nothing) shame – "*If I can't be perfect, then I must be completely worthless.*"

Shame and pride thus collude in a perpetual viscous cycle, one leading to more of the other, etc. As the cycle progresses, pride recreates shame, and then plans a fallacious means of healing the shame (striving for perfection), only to deepen the sense of shame when such attempts fail.

How, then can we become free from pride? I tell those I counsel that the tools of modern psychotherapy are valuable in helping us identify and eradicate shame. With the help of wise counsel, we can see that we were not originally born with an innate sense of shame, but that it developed in the mind of a child who concluded that disapproval from others was directly related to their unworthiness. Hopefully, we can understand from a more adult perspective that we do not cause others to hurt or reject us, but that such people are driven by their own internal sin (self-centeredness) and shame. We can now begin to see that since we are not fundamentally unworthy, we then do not need to strive for perfection as a means of achieving a sense of value and significance. Thus, we no longer "have to" become perfect. Yet our pride then kicks into gear and says, *"Yes, but I **want** to be perfect."* **Only through confession, repentance, and reliance upon the cleansing work of the Holy Spirit can I begin to be free from pride.**

What is commonly called "legalism" is a phenomenon driven by pride. Legalism is simply a term describing a person's attempts to achieve his own acceptability, his own value and identity, his own righteousness. Jesus warned his disciples not to follow in the footsteps of self-righteous Pharisees who actually added laws to the original Torah. The more laws, the higher the "mountain peak," and the more one could potentially prove one's acceptability to God and to other men. It is very significant to note that Jesus reserved his strongest language for the Pharisees, even calling them "sons of hell," (Matthew 23:15), which is as far as one could get from being "sons of righteousness."

Likewise, St. Paul had some very strong words for those who would add to the Gospel of Grace. In his letter to the Galatians, he warns the church of newborn Christians there not to fall prey to the theology of the "Judiazers." These were Jews, who claimed to believe that faith in Jesus' atoning death and resurrection was sufficient for salvation, but in fact, added the requirement of circumcision. **As soon as we add anything to faith alone in God's free gift of grace, then we negate grace.** It is in actuality a contradiction in terms to "add" anything to grace. Paul calls this an attempt to pervert the gospel of Christ (Galatians 1:7), and anyone who does so should be "eternally condemned" (vs. 9). Like Jesus, Paul expresses unmitigated anger towards those who would pervert the good news of pure grace. He states, as for those who would want to add the act of circumcision as a means of obtaining God's favor, "*I wish they would go the whole way and emasculate themselves*" (5:12). Could Paul have been any more blunt in expressing his feelings about the legalistic pride of this "circumcision group?"

For a longtime, I was puzzled about the statement Jesus made very early in his Sermon on the Mount. He says to his disciples something that must have been entirely foreign to their way of thinking: "*For I tell you that unless your righteousness surpasses that of the Pharisees and the teachers of the law, you will certainly not enter the kingdom of heaven*" (Matthew 5:20).

Imagine what must have been going through their minds – the Pharisees and their cohorts, the Scribes, who were the "professional," full-time keepers of the Law. How in the world could any ordinary Jew ever become more righteous? To make matters even more confusing, Jesus then goes on in the remainder of his sermon to explain how keeping the Law was even more difficult than anyone had thought. To truly keep the Law, one must be blameless not only in deeds, but also in attitudes and motives. Murder is not just a physical act; but the inner attitude of hatred is equivalent to killing a person in God's eyes. Neither is adultery simply a matter of crossing or violating a physical boundary; but any form of lust, whether or not it eventuates in sexual behavior is equivalent to doing so. In addition, Jesus' disciples are to love their enemies, when the basic requirement of the Law had been only to love one's neighbor.

Jesus blamed the Pharisees for placing an unbearable yoke upon the people; but at face value, his sermon would seem to break the necks of anyone attempting to follow him. The key to understanding Jesus' challenge to the disciples to surpass the righteousness of the Pharisees can be found in a previous verse: *"Do not think that I have come to abolish the Law and the Prophets; I have not come to abolish them but to fulfill them."* (5:17). Here is what Jesus meant: the only one whose righteousness could surpass that of the "professional" law-keepers was Jesus Himself. The only way that sinful and limited creatures could achieve such status would be by taking upon themselves the righteousness of Jesus. Only by being "clothed" with his righteousness, (Paul's terminology- Galatians 3:27), could human beings be viewed as being righteous in God's eyes.

Of course, under Jesus' covering, we still are, and always will be, sinners – in attitude, motives and deeds. Yet Jesus fulfilled the requirements of the Law by being perfect himself. Being the Perfect Lamb, He offered himself as an unblemished sacrifice to satisfy the Law's requirement of the death penalty for sin. Hence, ***Jesus is the Perfect Alibi...***Because he is perfect, we do not have to be.

Because He is perfect, He can perfectly atone for our prideful desires to be perfect ourselves without Him. He is the only legitimate alibi for not being perfect that we will ever need. Now, we can continue climbing up the mountains of life, negotiating its various challenges, setting goals and objectives for ourselves, without worrying how far our own efforts will take us. What is most amazing is that Jesus offers himself as our perfect alibi, purely out of his gracious love for us, knowing full well our imperfections and the depths of our sinfulness.

I trust that you, the reader, have begun to grasp the enormously wonderful implications of truly living by God's grace. We have been enslaved by the dynamics of psychological shame, and by our own prideful attempts to eradicate shame by achieving value and acceptability through our own efforts. What a tremendous burden is shed when we become freed from the "having to" and the "wanting to" strive for perfection. Philip Yancey refers to the "lightness of grace," in his book, *What's So Amazing About Grace?* (1997).

Another statement by Jesus has puzzled me most of my life as a Christian. In Matthew 11:28-30, Jesus encourages us to *"Come to me, all you who are weary and burdened, and I will give you rest. Take my yoke upon you and learn from me, for I am gentle and humble in heart, and you will find rest for your souls. For my yoke is easy and my burden is light."* This probably sounded idyllically nice to me as a young child when I added it to my collection of "memory verses." As I experienced more of life, however, I questioned how being a Christian could be "easy" when, in fact, many believers suffer tremendous persecution for their faith. Even those of us who are spared the threat of martyrdom face enough challenges to know that maintaining faith and hope in a loving God can be very difficult at times.

More recently, however, in my Christian pilgrimage, I have taken a different perspective on this passage, which I hope is indeed closer to the meaning intended originally by Jesus. He is not speaking about the Christian life being free from pain, suffering or other intense challenges. Instead, the "yoke" and "burden" that Jesus refers to are really his free gift of grace. Without such a gift, we are enslaved and burdened by others requirements; but more intensely, by our own requirements to live so perfectly that we could become fully acceptable to God, others and our own selves. **Grace is "light," because Jesus is our Perfect Alibi. We no longer experience the heavy burden of needing to strive for perfection, and we no longer need excuses when we fail.**

To return then to the question we asked a few pages back, how then can we be freed from our own pride? The theories and tools of modern psychotherapy can help heal the effects of shame, but only confession, repentance, and the work of the indwelling Spirit of God can begin to heal the effects of pride. During the previous generation, Paul Tournier, a Swiss medical doctor, pioneered some of the earlier attempts to integrate modern psychotherapeutic ideas with Biblical truth. He once said very succinctly, *"where psychotherapy ends, grace begins."*

The related fields of psychiatry and psychology represent humankind's attempts to diagnosis itself. Volumes upon volumes of theory and research have been somewhat helpful in categorizing and labeling all the things that can go wrong with mental processes, emotional states and relational functioning. However, these fields fall short in their understanding of the ultimate healing pathway for such pathologies.

To partake of God's grace, and to experience it at a level that goes beyond rational understanding alone, we must each first understand our need for it. At least two crucial steps are required. First, we must ask God to help us grasp the insidious depths of our prideful attempts to heal ourselves and to make ourselves acceptable by achieving perfection. I have reminded you more than once during his book that the unconscious mind does exist, and is very powerful, partly because it is by definition beyond our conscious awareness. As Jesus did in the Sermon on the Mount, we must also remind ourselves that sin originates at the level of attitudes and motives which are often unconscious (pride, lust, jealously, etc.). So first, we must humbly ask God to reveal to us the major ways in which our pride drives us towards perfection. Hopefully then, we can also see the ways in which we use "*mountain climber*" and "*base-camper*" techniques, and the various alibis that accompany them.

Awareness of such sin, as mentioned previously, should lead to a healthy, or godly sense, of brokenness, and then step two can occur – confession and repentance. Confession refers to the honest acknowledgement that we have sinned, and repentance means a deliberate turning around in a new direction away from the sin. I have found that it is much easier to consciously control my behavior than my attitudes. I can *act* as if I am not jealous, but I cannot actively control my attitudes and *feelings* of jealousy, or lust, or hatred, etc, (all of which can be subsumed under the general heading of pride, by the way). First, I need God to reveal to me my inner sins of pride, and then I can repent and ask for His forgiveness. Next, I must humbly ask God to fill me with the cleansing power of His Spirit, which is the means by which my pride begins to diminish.

Several years ago, God's still small voice made me painfully aware of my jealousy towards a friend. I was probably returning from an infrequent visit to this man's home where I noticed the growing discrepancy between his personal income and material possessions and my own. This discrepancy grew greater and greater over the years, at least as far as I could discern. On the surface, I assumed (perhaps this is my fantasy) that my jealousy was not noticeable. In fact, I was doing my best not to admit it to myself. Here, I think, was my logic: If I admitted to myself that I was jealous, then I would have to concede defeat. I had been competitive with this fellow in my mind, and thus prideful in my attempts to be better than him. While he surpassed me in income and material possessions, I self-righteously comforted my sense of shameful failure in those areas by asserting that I was devoting my life to more godly professional pursuits – helping others rather than "just making money." Do you see how pride and jealousy are related? I pridefully attempted to create and maintain my own sense of worth through my own endeavors, which I foolishly chose to see as superior to my friend's as well. In reality, I wished that I could have what he had and to achieve more of what the world, at least, defines as success. My pride fueled my jealousy – I wanted to have what he had in order to prove my value and worth, but if I couldn't, then I would need to believe that I was "better" than him in other ways.

Fortunately, basically, God said one day, *"Face it, son, you're jealous."* If I can recall correctly, this realization fortunately led to a sense of relief. There was something about "coming clean," about having the truth come out in the open; and it seemed to override any painful wound to my ego, which had fancied itself to be above the sin of jealousy.

Well, then, it was true – I was, and had been for many years – jealous of my friend. I now knew that I was jealous, and knew that God knew, and that He knew that I knew!

Somehow, I sensed God's Spirit saying to me that it was ok to be an imperfect sinner; God still loved me anyway. The fact that God had obviously known this about me all along, but had nonetheless been blessing me in many ways over the years, was a tremendous testimony to His gracious character. It is precisely through this process of revealing our sin to us, and expressing His continued desire to be in relationship with Him, that we move towards a natural and spontaneous praise and love of God in return. While I become convicted of my jealousy, and other sundry sins, I can choose to focus more on God and his character (as Peter did) rather than engage in self-focused denigration (as Judas apparently did).

There is a little more to the story of my jealousy, by the way. Once I became aware of my sinful attitude, I thanked God for his forgiveness, but then my pride kicked in to gear once more. I assumed that I could eradicate my jealousy through my own efforts. It was as if I were saying to God, "*Thank you for making me aware; now just give me a few weeks and I will take care of the problem. I'll just figure out a way to stop being jealous without Your help.*" Full of pride, I assumed that I had succeeded in this enterprise, until the next time I met my friend, or perhaps even heard about him through mutual acquaintances. Each new time his name was mentioned, I became aware that the jealousy had not simply evaporated. I finally figured out that I could not deliver myself from myself; I am a limited creature. And, that once again, God was patiently waiting for me to learn this fact first hand, so that He could then offer to empower me with His Spirit.

Slowly, I began to rely more upon God's Spirit to overcome my jealous attitude; and progressively, I achieved a degree of freedom. There was yet one more step in my "recovery," however. While I had begun to surrender the situation to God, I then assumed that His Spirit would magically, and immediately, evaporate the sin. Yet, as time progressed, I would occasionally notice that my jealousy, while minimized, still persisted. What happened? Had I not "surrendered" enough to God? Probably so, since we never do anything perfectly, and since my prideful spirit undoubtedly continued to thwart the working of God's cleansing Spirit. The issue was not a lack of power on God's part to effect complete cleansing within my heart, but rather that He never forcefully overrides our human will. Somewhere in the depths of my heart are prideful attitudes such as, "*I want to be better than my friend*," and/or, "*I want to get rid of my own prideful desires on my own.*"

The final (or at least what seems to be the final step at this point in my experience) step has been for me to begin thanking God for my friend. Why? Because, whenever I am reminded of my friend, I am likewise reminded of my jealousy, my inability to free myself from such sinful attitudes, and therefore my intense need for God's forgiveness and empowerment. In short, my friend reminds me of both my love for a God who loves me, a helpless and hopeless sinner, and my need for God. My love for Him and my neediness are what then propel me towards a deepened intimacy with Him, which is precisely what He most desires; and what in my heart of hearts I desire more than anything else in the world.

Just when I fool myself into believing that I have considered every possible way in which the Mountain of Perfection model can be applied, a current client comes along and broadens my understanding.

While attempting to put the finishing touches on this little book, I was counseling a woman who came to me because she simply could not keep her house in order. She freely admitted that her house had become tremendously cluttered with all kinds of items and that no matter how much she wanted to sift through, discard, and organize this pile of stuff, she perpetually procrastinated and the pile only continued to deepen. Oddly enough, she reported that she was quite responsible and organized in her workplace. In fact, cleaning was one of her part-time jobs that she did well. She even stated that she could help others clean their own homes and do so quite efficiently, but she could not bring herself to clean her own.

Now the roots of such a problem, like most problems, are probably multifaceted. However, after months of counseling sessions, my client made a statement that I believe exposed the core of the issue. Her comment went something like this: "If I do clean up my house, I don't know what I will do with myself." Often, procrastination (a *"base-camper"* technique) is fueled by the fear of unrealistically high expectations that will result if one actually achieves her original goal. If the Olympic runner does indeed win the gold medal, then he could easily expect himself to do the same four years later, and maybe even eight years hence. Knowing that this could be virtually impossible, the runner with such potential might simply procrastinate enough so that he never adequately prepares for the race, and thus falls short of the ideal goal (a form of self-sabotage).

In my client's case, I wondered if, in her subconscious mind, she feared the resultant expectations if she did succeed in cleaning her house completely – i.e., *"I must keep my house clean all the time to this degree."*

However, there is another reason why we sometimes avoid achieving our stated goal, and that is, in the depths of our soul, we realize that such success may not bring complete fulfillment. We have lived with the assumption that actual achievement of some ideal expectation or goal should bring a feeling of total fulfillment during our existence in this earthly life. **Perhaps nothing is more devastating than actually getting what we want, and finding out that it does not completely satisfy.**

One of my favorite movies of all times is *Chariots of Fire*, the story of Eric Liddell, an Olympic runner whose passion for competing and winning was surpassed only by his passion for God. The movie recounts the true story of the "Flying Scotsman," Eric, who uses the gift of swift feet to honor his God more than himself. At one point, he chooses not to violate the Sabbath Day by declining to run in the event that he was most sure to win. Instead, he preaches in a Scottish Presbyterian Church while the race is being run, and quotes the beautiful phrase from Isaiah 40:31, *"But those who hope in the Lord will renew their strength. They will soar on wings like eagles; they will run and not grow weary, they will walk and not be faint."*

A teammate graciously allows Eric to run in his place on the following day, in a race he was less prepared for. As always, he ran with his whole heart and not just his body, and indeed did take the gold medal.

The movie contrasts Eric with a young British runner, Harold Abrams, a gifted athlete and scholar, who ran against Eric prior to the 1927 Olympics, and then as a teammate on the combined team for Great Britain. While Eric viewed running as means of glorifying his Lord and Savior, Harold was compelled to prove to the world that his Jewish race was indeed not inferior to others. After WWI, anti-Semitism was beginning to mount throughout Europe, including the British Isles, and Harold was determined to show what God's *chosen people* could do.

I am sure that the Hollywood film makers were not intending to glorify or demean either Eric's or Harold's intensely strong passions for their respective religions. What eventually transpires is that both become winners on the track. Harold wins the race that Eric declined to run, and Eric gets the gold on the following day. Harold even wins the heart of a beautiful woman in the meantime. However, the movie portrays a stark contrast between the two. After Harold wins his race, he sits in a pub with his venerable trainer who expresses his joy over the win, and even his paternal love for the younger Harold. Harold responds with a sense of confusion, and even emptiness as he realizes that he has indeed achieved the long-sought-after goal. Having now accomplished all that he had lived for, he no longer knows where to turn or what to do to find fulfillment. In essence, he had made it to his self-contrived mountaintop, and upon doing so, realized that the promise of complete contentment had been false.

Eric is overjoyed as well, by his gold medal win, and celebrates with friends and family. However, it has been clear throughout the entire story that he was running as a means to an end versus running to win as an end in itself. The goal was to honor and glorify God. Perhaps the most pertinent line in the movie is when he explains to his sister that when Eric runs, he feels "*the pleasure of God.*" God had "*made me fast*" and he was only attempting to use that gift to its greatest extent for the Giver's sake, not for his own glorification. Thus, while winning was exhilarating, *what really brought pleasure to Eric was bringing pleasure to God.*

His career in this endeavor was just beginning. A documentary on the life of Eric after the Olympics, explains that he gave up his fame and fortune in Scotland, (he could have been the equivalent of a national sports hero like Michael Jordon in our country), and returned to China where his parents had been missionaries. While he was teaching in a missionary school, the Japanese invaded China and incarcerated Eric, along with the other faculty and all the students. He had left his wife and two daughters, and one on the way, in the safety of Canada.

Eric died of a brain tumor while interned in that prison camp, shortly after his 43rd birthday. Yet, the impact of his godly character touched many lives of those he taught and worked with, and his story continues to bring God glory to this day. He died, missing his wife and daughters tremendously; yet, with the contentment of having "*fought the good fight*" and "*finishing the race*" (II Timothy 4:7) for God's glory. Even the nurse at his bedside when he died testified to his love for God.

I am afraid that most of us have established mountain peaks in life other than the ultimate peak of living for God's honor and glory. The reason I have added this section to this chapter on *Freedom from Pride*, is that no matter how noble our goals might be, how humanitarian our efforts and motives might seem, **only what is done for God will satisfy, and only what is done for God will have lasting impact in this world and in eternity.** Anything short of this will undoubtedly leave us with emptiness and despair, as in the case of Harold Abrams. What could be any more devastating than having had a lifelong goal, achieving it, and then experiencing the gut-wrenching reality that it has not brought us fulfillment? In our pride, we assume that we know what will satisfy us, and how we can achieve it, independent of a relationship with our Creator. Once again, the only acceptable response is confession and repentance, and the acceptance of God's gracious love with which He desires to fill us. Let us not be like those to whom God referred when he said, *"These people come near to me with their mouth and honor me with their lips, but their hearts are far from me. Their worship of me is made up only of rules taught by men."* *(Isaiah 29:13)*

As we have done previously, let us conclude this chapter by returning to our two travelers, Alice and Ben. Alice, you recall, was the overly responsible and overly conscientious young woman who, since childhood, strove for perfection in all areas of life. Such a pursuit became the basis for her identity and purpose for living. We could argue that Alice was "victimized" by her family's situation (father's unavailability and her role as oldest of 5 kids), and that she naturally developed the shameful belief that her worth was tied to being perfectly responsible. However, it would also be the case that, just as any of us would do, Alice pridefully developed the desire to establish her worth and identity by completing tasks to please others.

As she entered into counseling, she could learn that she no longer had to live by such rules of approval, but hopefully, a wise and godly therapist would also gently confront her with her *desire* to play by such rules. Alice would then have the opportunity to turn to God with a humble attitude of confession and repentance, asking Him to free her from her own prideful attempts to be perfect. This process would then allow Alice, perhaps for the first time, to really begin to know God and His love for her. Probably, like many of us who glory in doing the "right things" in life, Alice knew much about God – through dutiful Scripture study and memorization, etc. – but had never really gotten to know Him in the context of an intimate relationship.

While she had developed a passion for doing the "right things" in life, she had not yet developed a passion for God Himself – a Person with whom she could have a direct relationship. God loves Alice so much that he allowed her to come to a breaking point, brought on by the stress created by shame and her prideful response to shame. Through the process of recovery, God breaks through the wall separating her from Him, and graciously convicts her of her sinful pride. As the Holy Spirit reveals to Alice her sinful attitudes, she then has the opportunity to receive God's forgiveness, just as the Apostle Peter did. This could then lead to a deepened awareness of her need for God, an increased love for Him who desires to fulfill that need, and a more intensely personal relationship with her Lord.

As to Alice coming to a point of crisis in her life, we all can identify, sooner or later, with that experience. While in the midst of the crisis, we all wonder whether God has abandoned us or is punishing us, or even whether our belief in God is itself well founded. However, here is something I have wondered about as I have the challenge and joy of guiding fellow Christians through periods of crisis: *Is it possible that God Himself wounds us, or at least allows the pain and suffering caused by evil to affect our lives, so that we can ultimately experience the more intense joy of "falling into" Him?* Were we never to be wounded and only experienced the relative pleasure of a comfortable life, we would then never experience the profoundly intense pleasure of knowing God and the rich depths of His love for us. Maybe the intense joy of being healed by God will someday more than justify the suffering, no matter how intense, that He has allowed to touch our lives.

As parents, we instinctively wish we could protect our children from any form of harm – physical, emotional, or relational trauma. Indeed, it is our God-given responsibility to protect helpless children as much as we can; but of course, we are limited in our attempts to achieve such a goal. Just imagine what the result would be, if we could achieve this goal perfectly. Our kids would be totally pain-free, totally content in their own worlds, with no need or appreciation for God whatsoever. What could be a worse evil than that? We worry about our children's safety in this life. Yet we know that just as God has done for us, He will, in His wisdom, allow them to face the pain of evil – at the hands of others, and due to their own sinfulness – so that they also can experience the riches of God's love; and thus know Him more intimately as they progress through life. This is why attempts to over-protect our children are pridefully sinful, based on the assumption that we know better than God does what course their lives should take.

Finally, we can see the results of pride in the life of our young traveler, Ben. While Ben felt inferior to his older brothers and incapable of attaining heights of success similar to theirs, his pride "piggy-backed" on this sense of personal shame, creating a desire to do as well, if not better than them, in order to command the respect and approval of family and friends. Especially in a person as young as Ben (high school age), such prideful attitudes would be buried in his subconscious; but nonetheless, it would still be there, within his heart and mind. His "logic of shame" would have stated, *"You must be as successful as your brothers in order to be acceptable to others and to yourself."* In reply, the *"logic of pride"* would add, *"Yeah, and wouldn't I be great if I could equal or even surpass the others – then I could really show them I am somebody. I want to be as good as, and even better, than my brothers."* However, Ben then finds himself in a trap: *"No matter how hard I try, I could never be that successful. My best efforts would only be mediocre, and then I couldn't live with myself. So, it makes more sense not to try my best, and be criticized as a result – but that's better than finding out that my best is not good enough"* (i.e., perfect.).

If Ben is able to understand through some wise counsel, that he does not have to be like his brothers, and that he can be valued for who he is, apart from the quality of his performance, then his shame would begin to dissipate. Such insights tend to come more easily when young people move into adulthood. Adults simply have a greater capacity for self-awareness than a teenager generally would have. Others can help the teenager by graciously loving them along with their relative flaws and inadequacies.

Eventually, then, after Ben would begin to realize that he does not *have* to be perfect, he would also need God's loving Spirit to convict him of his prideful *desire* to be perfect. As he matured, by focusing more upon God's character - His complete perfection - then Ben would be freed to give any challenge in life his best effort, using whatever gifts, skills and resources God has given him. He would no longer need to scrutinize how well or not so well he was performing in regards to standards in any and all areas of life, because what would matter most is not himself anyway, but Christ alone. Being drawn to Christ, Ben would naturally become more Christ-like in his ways of relating to people, without him even being aware of the changes that would be occurring in his character.

Chapter 7:

Freedom to Love God and Others

"For in Christ Jesus neither circumcision nor uncircumcision has any value. The only thing that counts is faith expressing itself through love." (Galatians 5:6)

The fundamental problem with both the *"mountain-climber"* and *"base-camper"* approaches to life is that the focus of attention is primarily upon one's self. If one attempts to climb the mountains that he has created, then there ensues a constant and vigilant scrutiny of one's progress: *How well am I doing? What if I slip and fall down the mountain? Now that I have achieved a particular peak, can I manage the next higher "peak" that I demand and desire to conquer?* Even if our mountain peak were to be "perfect godliness", we would be checking our progress on a regular basis to see just how "godly" we are. This, of course, is a contradiction in terms. True godliness involves a "loss of self," a kind of self-forgetfulness because our eyes are upon God Himself, rather than upon our own progress.

The *"base-camper,"* while perhaps pretending not to care about climbing mountain peaks, also engages in self-focus. She, at least unconsciously, if not consciously as well, is quite aware of her shame-based need and pride-driven desire to be at the top of a particular peak, but lives with the depressive self-blame of not being there. Denial is the defense mechanism of preference in this case: If I can convince myself and others, that I don't care about achieving any particular goals or objectives in life, then I can pretend that the mountain peak doesn't even exist – *"Mountain? What mountain? Oh, that one...well, you know, I don't really care about it anyway."* Then I can go about life simply focusing upon what makes me comfortable, and does not threaten my self-made world of avoidance.

As one begins to heal from the pain of shame, and to be freed from the prideful drive towards perfection, negotiating mountains is no longer a problem. Rather than frenetically scrambling up the mountain, or phobically avoiding the challenge of climbing, we can set reasonable goals for our lives and move towards them without fear of failure. Realizing that perfection is neither necessary (since Jesus is perfect *for me*) nor attainable (God created me as a limited creature), we can give life our "best shot" on any given day, and not be concerned with how flawless our performance may or may not be. We can strive for excellence in all that we do, precisely because we are not attempting to perform perfectly. Like Eric Liddell, we can run the races in life only to "*feel God's pleasure,*" and not to satisfy our self-made demands for flawlessness. Like, Eric, **we can now strive for excellence rather than perfection.**

Excellence is not synonymous with perfection, though many of us do equate the two in our minds. Excellence involves working hard and tenaciously to perform at increasingly high levels of performance. Yet, no matter how well one performs at a given time, there is always room for improvement. This is not the same, however, as saying, "*enough is never enough*" or "*no matter how hard I try it isn't good enough.*" Such clichés reflect the **logic of perfectionism.**

The **logic of excellence** accepts the fact that no performance is ever perfect, but that reality does not threaten our value, worth and acceptability as a person. *Since I no longer need nor desire to be perfect, I can truly try my hardest in every task I undertake, and not worry about how far up the mountain my progress takes me.* We may achieve a certain height one day, and then slip back to a lower height the next. The fact is we are not primarily concerned with our level of performance when we live by grace, because our focus of attention has shifted from us to God.

If we can imagine a *grace-filled* mountain climber setting out on his journey, we would see him gazing at the peak as he climbs. At the peak is Jesus, the ***Perfect Alibi.*** No other alibis are needed in case the climber fails, because failure is measured against perfection, and the grace-based climber has allowed Christ to be perfect for him, releasing himself from the burden of flawlessness.

The godly, *"grace-filled climber"* does indeed set goals for himself. He does desire to use the gifts and abilities with which God has endowed him to fulfill the roles and related tasks that God has assigned to him.   He does want to become an excellent father, professional, husband, friend, and spiritually mature disciple of Christ. *Excellence in all these areas of life is ultimately understood to be Christ- likeness.*   Thus, as he gets up in the morning to play these various roles, his primary focus is on the Person and Character of his Lord and Savior, who of course reflects the glory of God the Father. His goal is to grow closer to Christ and the Father, through the empowerment of the Holy Spirit. *His greatest passion is to know God and in so doing, to become like him and reflect his glory to the world around him.*

The *"mountain-climbers"* and *base-campers"* are rather fascinated with themselves – either positively (*"Look how high I can climb by myself!"*) or negatively (*"What a loser I am – I can't climb for beans"*). In contrast, the *"grace-filled" climber* is increasingly fascinated with God.

We become most like the thing or person that we worship. A young boy with a passion for baseball determines who his favorite professional player is. If he is really enamored by his hero, he will want to dress like him, talk and act like him, and certainly play ball like him. In short, he wants to become just like him in every way possible. Likewise, the true grace-filled disciple of Jesus will not only want to bear his name ("Christian"), but act like him and be like him in every way possible.

The baseball fan learns everything he can about his hero; the Christian strives to know more and more about his Hero, Jesus. The baseball fan would love most of all, to personally know his hero and have close relationship with him; the Christian is not content with facts and data about his Hero, but intensely desires to have an intimate relationship with him. **Knowing God, through His Son, Jesus, becomes the final and highest goal of the *grace-filled climber*; not flawless perfection.** While Jesus was and is perfect in every sense of the word, the *grace-filled climber* is not attempting to be complete and flawless in the same way. Rather than attempting to duplicate the perfection of Christ, he or she is striving for an increasingly close relationship with the person of Christ.

As *grace-filled climbers* negotiate their mountains in life, they are less aware of how well they are progressing, and more aware of Christ at the peak. He is like a magnet, drawing them towards Him. With the author of Hebrews they exclaim, *"Let us fix our eyes on Jesus, the author and perfecter of our faith..."* (Hebrews 12:2*)*.   In fact, the context of that verse in Hebrews 12 includes the warning that the Christian journey is often difficult. We, like Christ, face opposition from "sinful men" and we struggle with our own sin. These are the rocks, crags, and steep places on our mountain paths. However, by keeping our focus on Christ we are able to negotiate these challenges, freed to do our best, empowered by the Holy Spirit; and also, free to slip and fall.

The Old Testament says, *"For though a righteous man falls seven times, he rises again."* (Proverbs 24:16).*"* The passage does *not* state, *"If* the righteous man falls," or *"If* a man is truly righteous, he will not fall.*"* Inevitably, a sinful and limited man will "fall." Yet, falling and being unrighteous are not synonymous because our righteous is not our own – it is Christ's. This means we are still acceptable to God and our value to Him remains intact whenever we fall.

How can we maintain our focus upon Christ and strive for excellence as we use the gifts and resources that He has given us? How can we stop obsessing upon how well or poorly we think we are doing and become more amazed at how perfectly loving, glorious, gracious and powerful God is? I believe that we begin the transfer from self-focus to God-focus when we realize how sinful and dependent we are, and how marvelously gracious God is to continue gifting us with his un-merited favor. The more aware I become, (with the Holy Spirit's help), of the depth of my pride, and its passion for building mountains and *peaks of perfection*, the more I have the opportunity to grasp the depths of God's love for me. I often tell clients that **Christian maturation is not primarily a process of becoming less and less sinful, but rather a process of becoming progressively more aware of the depth and intensity of my sinfulness, and my corresponding need for Christ's righteousness.** Humility before God is the goal of maturation much more so than prideful attempts to become acceptable by my own efforts.

As I have done more than once in this book, I refer the reader to the works of Dr. Larry Crabb. His 1988 work, *Inside Out*, is perhaps the most powerful book I have come across in my lifetime, in terms of teaching us about the nature and depth of sin. Dr. Crabb simply echoes the challenge that Jesus Himself gave to the listeners of His "Sermon on the Mount:" Be aware of sinful attitudes and motives, which underlie behaviors, as opposed to assuming that "right" behaviors are enough. As Jesus said to the self-righteous Pharisees, *"You clean the outside of the cup and dish, but inside they are full of greed and self-indulgence. Blind Pharisees! First clean the inside of the cup and dish, and then the outside also will be clean."* (Matthew 23: 25-26). Dr. Crabb masterfully delineates various ways in which we subtly sin on the attitudinal level; and thus I highly recommend his book, along with the many others he has written over the course of his career. I would take the liberty of summarizing his teaching on sin, by narrowing it all down ultimately to pride.

Whether it may be through Dr. Crabb's writings, the works of other fine authors, or of course, Scripture itself, we all need to ask God to reveal to us the subtle, but insidious, depths of our pride. Self-awareness, however, is not God's primary goal for us, but is only another means to a greater end, that being to spur our hearts towards God. **The more we know about our sin, the more we can see our need for Christ and His righteousness; and the more we are amazed by a God who graciously loves us, in spite of our prideful attempts at self-righteousness.**

In other words, the more we know about God's love for us, the more we strive to love Him in return, and the more we love Him, *the more we will love others*, which is what this final chapter is all about. Being freed from both shame and pride, we are now free to love others, as Christ would have us love them.

Being raised in a Christian environment, with a strong emphasis on learning facts and data about God, it was not until adulthood that I began to grasp the fact that ***Truth is relational more than*** *propositional*. Truth with a capital "T" is God, and understood by us through His Son, Jesus. Truths, with a small "t" are statements, facts, data about God, which being derived from the inspired words of God (Scripture) tell us much about His being and character. Yet such "propositional truths" are meant to lead us to a relationship with the Truth as a Person. A person can *believe* in the basic data about God, but it is through *faith* that one moves from the knowledge *about* God to a knowledge *of* God. The link between belief and faith involves the risk of trusting in God's love, grace, and provision for our lives, which is ultimately expressed through the process of loving our fellow creatures. As the prophet, Habakkuk (2:4) reminds us, *"The righteous will live by his faith."* Paul extends this by telling his Galatian readers, and us, *"For in Christ Jesus neither circumcision nor uncircumcision has any value. The only thing that counts is faith expressing itself in love."* (Galatians 5:6).

Obviously, one small chapter in one small book cannot do justice to the depths of what it means to love God by loving others. My specific goal, as we finish off this *"Mountain of Perfection"* model is to discuss love in the context of the relational challenges that my clients bring to my office, which are ones that we all face as well. Since Truth is relational, then we should strive to have loving relationships with both our Lord and our fellow life-travelers.

To begin, let me say that the term, *"love,"* is probably one of the most poorly understood and often-misused words in the English language by our modern culture. Love in our popular culture is usually understood to mean a positive feeling towards another. Spouses often tell me that they no longer "love" their husband or wife, by which they nearly always mean they do not *feel* attracted to them anymore. Romantic love, or *"falling in love,"* is glorified in our youth-oriented culture as the glue that holds a relationship together, and once it has softened, the relationship will fall apart unless such feelings can be rekindled. The problem, as many Christians already know, is that when we translate the New Testament from its original Greek into English, we use the word "love" to convey what at least three separate Greeks words intend to express. The Greek language used the word, *"eros"* to describe the physical passion that often attracts people together. The term, *"philios"* referred to "brotherly" affection and kindness.   However, what the New Testament writers, and Jesus Himself, spoke most frequently and earnestly about was *"agape,"* or committed love. "Agape" love is the self-sacrificial love that Jesus demonstrated so perfectly, always putting the legitimate needs of others before His own.

In a marriage, it is that kind of love that spurs the husband to serve his wife and family, as Christ lovingly served His Bride, the Church. In return, it is that kind of love that inspires a wife to serve or "submit" willingly to her Christ-like husband (Ephesians 5). While a healthy marriage does involve "philios" and "eros", its foundation is built on "agape" love.   Other types of relationships (parent-child, mutual friendships, siblings, business relationships, and relationships within the church community, and even relationships with perfect strangers) involve varying degrees of philios, but all should involve agape love.

I like to explain "agape" love in this manner: ***"True love involves anything that we say or do, or in some cases not say or do, that either encourages or challenges the other partner(s) to become more Christ-like themselves."***   Sometimes we make sacrifices on the behalf of others, and sometimes we say loving and encouraging words that build up and strengthen one's commitment to Christ.   In other circumstances, it is more loving not to do or say certain things, because to do so would hinder the partner's journey towards Christ-like maturity.   A Biblical basis for this expression of love is found in Ephesians 4.   A prominent theme in Paul's letter to the Ephesian church is that of unity: *"Make every effort to keep the unity of the Spirit through the bond of peace"* (vs. 3).   Paul uses the phrase, *"speaking the truth in love"* (vs. 15) in the context of this goal of unity.   As less mature believers fall prey to deceitful teaching and revert to their *"former way of life"* (vs. 22), those who are more mature are to lovingly challenge them to be more Christ-like. They do so by *"speaking the truth"* in love.

While *"truth"* here could mean correct doctrine about the Truth, Christ Himself, I believe it refers more in this context, to the reality that a brother or sister is straying from such doctrine in his behaviors or attitudes.   The term *"truth"* may not always refer to objective facts either. It may be my perception that a brother is failing in his Christian walk, but I may not have all the facts. Yet, it is *true* that I am concerned about my brother based on what I have heard or observed. Unity in the church can only occur as members lovingly encourage and challenge one another towards Christ-like maturity.

When we observe the lack of Christ-likeness in another, we tend to respond in the direction of either one extreme or the other. On one hand, many of us *fail to speak truth, thinking that to do so is loving.* We assume that to be honest with someone who is hurting others and himself, is "mean" and hurtful to them. In reality, our motives are very self-centered. We don't want to be hurt by their defensive response if we confront them. Hence, dishonesty in such situations is *not* truly loving, because it is more self-focused than other-directed.

The opposite extreme, as you can imagine, involves attacking others with the reality of their wrongdoing. When we are in this mode, we *may speak the truth, but not lovingly.* My wife once worked for a university president who was indeed a brilliant man with keen insight. He knew which professors were diligent scholars and which were in essence slackers. However, when he confronted the latter group, he did so with a verbal lambasting which demeaned not only their performance but their personhood as well. Obviously, this approach towards others is not loving either, and is equally self-centered because it presumably allows us to feel better by "venting" our thoughts and feelings.

In between these two extremes is the balance point achieved by *speaking the truth in love.* In this mode, we are honest about our observations, feelings, perceptions that have occurred in response to a fellow Christian's behavior. It may sound something like this: *"Tom, I don't know for sure, but it seemed to me that you were being quite critical in last night's committee meeting. I care enough about you and our relationship to let you know that I felt hurt. I want to discuss this further with you so that we can continue the great friendship we have had, rather than just sweep the incident under the rug."* This is an honest statement, based on perception more than fact, but still honest. It is loving because its intent is the maturation of Tom and the enhancement of my relationship in Christ with him. How Tom responds, by the way, is his issue, his responsibility; but if I speak the truth and do so lovingly, he will be less apt to be defensive and more prone towards reconciliation. Once again, Paul sums it up this way: *"Therefore each of you must put off falsehood and speak truthfully to his neighbor, for we are all members of one body"* (4:25).

As we become increasingly fascinated with God, rather than with ourselves, our natural response is to mirror His graciousness to our fellow creatures. The harder we are on ourselves, the harder we are on others; the more we expect of ourselves, the more we expect of others. If I expect myself to be a perfect father, by definition, I must have perfect children. Fortunately, the reverse is also true. The more gracious and loving I am towards myself, the more I can graciously accept others and their imperfections. As the Apostle Paul has said, "The man who loves his wife loves himself," and by logical implication, the reverse would also be true - a healthy self-love leads to a healthy, gracious acceptance of others.

This graciousness is a component of *agape* love because we are communicating to others the same unconditional, unmerited love that God demonstrates towards us. Accepting people for *"who they are"* as opposed to *"what they do"* is grace. The opposite of this would be expressed by the father, who removes his love from his son because the son's academic performance slides, and he no longer makes the father proud. On the other hand, what about the husband who leaves his wife after a few children and several years of marriage for a younger, more physically appealing woman (erotic love)? The worst story I have ever heard along these lines is of the husband whose wife of many years contracted cancer and he abandoned her, because he could no longer derive pleasure from her. A Christ-like husband would instead dive into encouraging, compassionate service to his ailing wife, mirroring the sacrifice that Jesus has made for them both.

Genuine and mature Christ-like love is too often confused, however, with *"codependent"* ways of relating. This modern "pop" psychology term, *"codependency,"* can be best defined as a self-centered drive, in fact an addiction, towards winning others approval. It is the pride-based means that most of us employ to satisfy our need and desire for significance and to compensate for shame. On the surface, the strongly codependent person appears to be very loving and other-focused, but beneath that veneer is the self-centered motive of pleasing others in order to feel good about himself. He will make what seems to be phenomenal sacrifices for others, but with the underlying (and usually unconscious) motives of proving his value and worth to others and to himself.

I think all but a very small percentage of us do indeed depend too much upon gaining the approval of others. (Remember the most negatively powerful "*rule of approval?*" It is that I expect myself to live up to everyone else's expectations of me). In our attempt to gain our sense of self, we actually lose it. We become divorced from our own legitimate wishes, needs, desires, preferences, and in essence, don't know who we are. I once heard an overstated but very apt definition of this whole state of affairs: "*You know you are codependent when you are drowning, and someone else's life flashes before your eyes!*" You become so focused on feeling better about yourself, by attempting to meet others' needs and desires, that you lose touch with the legitimate aspects of your unique personhood.

In contrast, Philippians 2 explains the model for the kind of love we are called to express: Christ, being divine, laid aside the rights and powers associated with his divinity (but not his actual divinity), and then chose to enter into human form to suffer on our behalf. Jesus knew who he was, and was well aware of the respect to which he was entitled. Yet, he consciously and deliberately chose to make profound sacrifices on our behalf. The classic codependent stance is quite different. Due to a strong sense of inner shame, an individual does not have a well-developed sense of self, and looks to others for completion. One cannot engage in self-sacrifice until she is first aware that she has a legitimate self. *You have to have a self before you can give it away.* In codependent relationships, a person may perform what appears to be loving acts of service, but the underlying motive is actually rather self-centered: "*I will do whatever you want me to do, so that I can win your approval, which I need in order to begin loving myself.*"

I like to tell clients that **we are called to love others; not to please them** - a simple, but very profound distinction. Christ-like love is always directed towards the primary good of the other, rather than being driven by self-interest. *The primary good for others is ultimately that they grow into Christ-likeness themselves.* Thus, **mature Christ-like love is always other-centered rather than self-centered**. With this goal in mind, our love towards others can take two primary forms: One is the encouraging, compassionate, go-the-extra-mile, form of love, which is appropriate when someone has a legitimate need that cannot be fulfilled without assistance. The other form is the challenging, admonishing, "speaking-the-truth-in-love" (Ephesians 4:15) side of love that is called for when others are not owning responsibility for their own thoughts, feelings and actions.

A common example would be the situation in which the classically codependent wife must have a Judge serve her abusive husband with a restraining order. I suggest to such clients that their primary intent must be to challenge their husbands to move towards Christ-like maturity, rather than simply to stand up for themselves, make their lives easier, or even protect their children. These are healthy by-products of loving assertiveness, but should not be the wife's primary goal. Again, Christ-like love by definition always seeks the goal of directing and challenging others towards a deepened love for, and relationship with, Christ. As Paul says to Titus (2:15), "encourage *and* rebuke..."

Mature Christ-like love is always "risk-taking" in nature. As a wife challenges her husband to acknowledge and seek help for his addiction, she runs the risk of incurring his wrath and perhaps even being abandoned by him. The latter is especially threatening to a woman whose sense of self is so wounded that she would rather be physically abused by a man who is with her, than to lose any form of attention from him. However, ***God calls us to love others to such an extent that we may even risk losing our relationship with them*** (just as is the case with Christ and all of humanity). Many parents are afraid of "losing" their children's love and affection if they set firm limits upon them. For people in my profession, who need to attain continuing education credits to maintain our mental health licenses, a recent seminar about "over-indulged" children and the parents who enable them has become quite popular. (I chuckle to myself when I see this advertised because I think my own profession is largely at fault for encouraging parents a generation ago to be more "tolerant" and accepting of children's wishes and desires).

When we fail to offer appropriate encouragement and compassion to others, we miss the opportunity to teach them the unconditional love of Christ. When a child fails to perform to a expected standards, but her parents show concern and respect for her unique personhood, that child learns that she is loved, period; not loved only if...if she performs or pleases, etc. We saw in the early chapters of this book what happens when a child perceives that certain "rules of approval" must be followed before he or she can feel acceptable to others and to themselves. As an employer, I often fail to encourage and "come along side" my staff. I tend to get into my own busy world and assume that the therapists under my supervision only need my direction when they have a specific question to ask me, or when I think they need a challenge to perform more professionally. We should not overlook the importance of helping, serving, encouraging, and caring for others as a means of teaching them about Christ, so that they can grow into further Christ-likeness themselves.

One significant expression of such "encouraging" love is forgiveness. Since we have all been hurt by someone, at some time in our lives, then we all have the opportunity to forgive. Extending forgiveness is an act of grace, just as God has extended His forgiveness to us. Paul tells the Ephesians, *"Be kind and compassionate to one another, forgiving each other, just as in Christ God forgave you"* (4:32). As we receive God's forgiveness, as did the Apostle Peter, it means we have decided to forgive ourselves for legitimate wrongdoing and unloving attitudes on our own parts. Having been gracious in this way towards ourselves, we are then more apt to be graciously forgiving towards others. We no longer expect perfection of them, because we do not expect it of ourselves.

Forgiveness is a process. It begins with the conscious choice to no longer hold the offender accountable for his or her harmful words or actions; and it continues on, so that with each future reminder of the offense, we can choose to forgive or not to forgive. Many excellent books have been written on this crucial subject, and my favorites are by the writer, Lewis Smedes (1988, 1996). Rather than attempt in this brief chapter to summarize all that Smedes and others in the Christian community have stated so well in their own works, I trust that the motivated reader will seek out these other sources. I will make a few pertinent points about the process of forgiveness. First, it **requires the empowerment of the Holy Spirit.** When we have been intensely hurt, it may be that we cross a threshold beyond our God-given capacity to forgive. On the other hand, it may be that we are trapped by our own unwillingness to forgive, and our corresponding inability to overcome our unwillingness. Either way, we need God to give us the *desire* and the *power* to forgive.

As usual, our **pride can be a hindrance to forgiveness**, because we see ourselves as more righteous than the one who has hurt us. As we allow the Holy Spirit to lovingly convict us, then He can gently, but clearly, remind us of our own sinfulness, and our own need for His forgiveness. Then, we will have greater motivation to forgive others when we see that we are really in the "same boat" as they are. Take for example the survivor of serious childhood abuse. When she recognizes that while the abuse was clearly not her fault, but sees that she has responded in pride-driven ways to heal her own shame, then she is more apt to ask God for the desire and power to forgive the sin of her perpetrator.

How do we know, however, when such an "encouraging love" is appropriate, and when a more "challenging" form of agape love is called for? A simple "rule of thumb" is this: **Help others only to the extent that they are unable to help themselves. Otherwise, challenge them to do for themselves what they indeed are capable of doing.** A person with a strong "dose" of codependency will do things for others that they should be doing for themselves. In explaining this to a mother of a teenaged son, I asked if she could imagine a mother tying the shoes of a 15 year old. I knew we had some serious work to do when she blushed and after a few seconds said, "*Well, only certain pairs.*" In fact, her attempt to "*love*" her son by doing such tasks actually gave him a very unloving message: "*I do not believe that you are, or ever will be, capable of living without me.*" She had the proverbial "*need to be needed*" (another definition of codependency), which spurred her towards "*over-doing*" for others.

People who do too much for others are, by definition, attracted to people who do too little for themselves. *Overly responsible people mate with those who are under-responsible.* It is incredible, but highly predictable, the way that such people are unconsciously attracted to one another. They each live according to the myth that self-fulfillment can be found in what someone else can do for them. Classically, the wife in such a marriage plays the overly responsible role, and the husband plays the under-responsible role. They both assume that if she just works hard enough at it, she can complete his inadequate sense of self by doing whatever he wants, whenever he wants it. In turn, she assumes that if she can complete this impossible task, she will feel fulfilled in having played by the rules of her role as the overly responsible partner.

Likewise, children assume that parents are responsible for their happiness and fulfillment, and parents who agree with this assessment over-indulge their children and wonder why the more they do for them, the more their children want, and the less grateful they are. This can happen in any relational setting (businesses, churches, friendships) in which both parties assume that one party is primarily responsible for the emotional well-being of the other.

What actually does develop, however, is what we call *"hostile-dependent"* relationships. The mother who does too much for her son now has a teenager who hates her for continuing to communicate through her behavior towards him that he is inadequate, and he hates himself for being inadequate. Yet, feeling inadequate, he fears that he must remain dependent upon her. Therefore, a vicious cycle ensues. He may eventually break away from his mother's apron strings, but then transfers his dependency upon a girlfriend or wife. Again, this can occur in churches and other organizations in which the leadership does too much for the rank-and-file members, who grow dependent upon the leaders and learn to despise themselves and the leaders. The leaders' usual response is, *"How can you be so ungrateful? Don't you know how much we have done for you?"*

Instead of this false, counterfeit attempt to be loving, *true agape love always challenges the other party to be more responsible for themselves.* By the way, this not only includes physical acts and responsibilities such as tying one's shoes, but also assuming ownership of one's own thoughts, feelings, attitudes, motives, wishes, desires. In other words, everything that goes on in each of our own hearts and minds. Our human tendency is to make others responsible for our thoughts, feelings, and actions. The abusive boyfriend pretends to apologize when he says he is sorry to his girlfriend for having hit her last night and then adds, *"but you should know that I don't like my apple pie with ice cream on it."* While I have never actually heard a statement quite this blunt, I have heard many family members attempt to make others responsible for their own distress and their own inappropriate behavior.

The plain fact of the matter is no one *"makes"* us think, feel, or act a certain way, and neither can we compel other people to think, act, or feel in a certain way. Each of us *chooses* how we will think, feel and act in response to life events and others' actions towards us.

A major component of Christ-like maturity is the humble willingness to accept **responsibility for myself** (my thoughts, my feelings, my desires, my actions, etc.). A related component involves being **responsible to others**. This includes carrying out agreed upon commitments (such as fulfilling my duties on the job, faithfully preparing each week to teach the Sunday School class that I signed up for, etc.) and challenging others to do the same. As a godly father, one of my responsibilities *towards* my children is to encourage and challenge them to be responsible for themselves so they will not grow up learning to blame others for their irresponsible choices. As the director of a counseling center, I have certain responsibilities *towards* my staff, while not being responsible *for* them.

While we need to be **responsible for ourselves** and **responsible to others**, we are clearly not to be **responsible for others.** The latter suggests that it is our job to *"make"* them happy and to guarantee their emotional, physical and spiritual well-being. Whenever we begin to live within the boundaries of these forms of responsibility, those who tend towards under-responsibility become angry and resentful, at least to begin with. Eventually, if they choose to stay in relationship with us (and they may not), they will understand that we have indeed loved them through both encouragement and challenge.

Christ certainly loves us enough to risk losing a relationship with us. He wants only a particular kind of relationship, based on our desire to respond to His loving sacrifice on our behalf. He does not need a relationship with us; rather He wants us to want Him, which is the only basis for a healthy connection. However, by allowing us the freedom to choose to draw near to Him, by definition He also allows us the freedom to withdraw and run away. We must approach our own human relationships in the same manner. *Christ-like love is therefore quite risky, but anything short of that is not real love anyway.*

Let us return to forgiveness for a minute: In abusive relationships, ***forgiveness is often confused with tolerance.*** The classically co-dependent girlfriend assumes that forgiving her boyfriend for abusing her means allowing him back into her life with no consequences, which only communicates to him that he can hurt her again. On the contrary, forgiveness is an act that occurs in the heart and mind of the offended, and is not contingent upon the behavior of the offender. If the offender persists once we have begun to forgive, then the loving response on our part is to continue to apply consequences and set appropriate limits. I once knew a man whose son was killed by a drunk driver. At the court trial, he told the driver that he forgave him but still intended to press charges and see that justice was done. Applying appropriate consequences communicates the message that *"I love you enough to do whatever is in my power to challenge you to never hurt me or anyone else like this again – because for you to continue doing so demeans your personhood as well as that of your victims."*

Along these same lines, ***forgiveness is not to be equated with reconciliation.*** A common misunderstanding is that we cannot forgive our perpetrator unless he or she admits that they have hurt us and is legitimately sorry for their offense. No, once again, forgiveness occurs within our own heart and mind. As we extend it to another, we can continue forgiving no matter how they respond. If they are indeed penitent, then we can work towards reconciliation, but the lack of reconciliation does not impede our process of forgiveness.

One final note about forgiveness: ***The only alternative is bitterness.*** I was once asked to speak to an adult Sunday School class on the specific topic of bitterness. As I prepared to teach that lesson, I first scanned through various psychiatric and psychological dictionaries, confirming what I had already assumed, which is that the term is never used. Strange in a way, because it can cause so much devastation to one's body and psyche. A quick glance through any Bible concordance, however, reveals scores of verses mentioning bitterness. As I read through them, I found a strong theme: Bitterness, if not healed, will eat us from the inside out. The only means of healing bitterness is to forgive, and the only real way to forgive is to take the risk of trusting that God will give us the means and power to do so.

The only reason why someone would engage in such risk-taking love is out of love, obedience and faith towards God - a God who promises to honor our dependence upon Him, no matter what the costs may be for us. Therapists who counsel people in the throes of codependency often suggest that their clients become more assertive. In their effort to win others' approval, such folks usually allow others to *"walk all over them"* and take advantage of their dependency. A misguided solution to this situation is for those with codependent tendencies to practice becoming more assertive. *"Stand up for yourself; stop letting others run rough-shod over you. You need to assert your rights, your wishes, and your ideas."*

Instead, the solution for codependency is not to become more assertive for the sake of feeling better about yourself; but to love others in a way that both encourages and challenges others to become more Christ-like themselves. Again, we are called to love others, and not just to please them. However, as we do so, an amazing paradox occurs - in *"losing"* ourselves in such love for others, we truly begin to *"find ourselves."* What we call *"positive self-regard"* or *"heightened self-esteem"* should never be our primary goal. Instead, loving others as a faithful act of obedience to our Lord and Savior is our highest calling. A healthy self-love then gradually develops, outside of our conscious awareness, as a secondary bi-product of this calling.

Having been freed from shame, we no longer need to worry that a failure to please others will only increase our self-denigration. Moreover, as we become increasingly freed from pride, we are no longer driven by the desire to win others' approval, and the only desire we have, like the Apostle Paul is *"to know...Jesus Christ and Him crucified."* (1 Corin.2:3). We are then freed to love others with the same love by which Christ has loved us. Having grown closer to Christ, we are filled with the passionate desire for others to grow in the same manner. We move ahead in our relational worlds with the wisdom of the Holy Spirit, who helps us discern when to encourage and when to challenge, and gives us the power to do both.

We find our fulfillment, meaning and purpose in life through knowing that God has loved us enough, each of us consummate sinners, to use us as His instruments to communicate His Grace to others. Finally, as we attempt to love in our limited ways, we have no need to do so flawlessly, because Christ Himself is our *Perfect Alibi.*

The most satisfying experience I have ever had in my professional life so far has probably been when one client in her last session simply said, *"You have taught me about God's grace."* I can only hope that my family and closest friends could say this about me someday, and even more that each of them, and you, the reader, can have this same satisfaction of knowing that God has been using you to extend His Kingdom of Grace.

Set reasonable goals for the development of the roles that He has placed you in and for the expression of the gifts with which God had endowed you. Strive indeed for excellence, but do not fear falling short of your ideals. The highest ideal is the humility associated with our need and love for Christ. Realize that *"growing in grace"* is a process. Be gracious towards yourself, as God is towards you, when you become aware that shame and pride have caused you to temporarily slide back down the mountainside.

"But grow in the grace and knowledge of our Lord and Savior Jesus Christ. To him be glory both now and forever! Amen" (2 Peter 3:18).

References:

Benner, David G. (1998). *Care of souls: Revisioning Christian nurture and counsel.* Grand Rapids, Michigan: Baker Books.

Bryson, Bill. (1998). *A walk in the woods.* New York, NY: Broadway Books.

Crabb, Lawrence J. (1988). *Inside out.* Colorado Springs, CO: NavPress.

Crabb, Lawrence J. (1993). *Finding God.* Grand Rapids, Michigan: Zondervan.

May, Gerald. (1988). *Addiction & grace.* New York, NY: Harper & Row Publishers.

McGee, Robert S. (1990). *The search for significance.* Houston, Tx: Rapha.

Smedes, Lewis. (1984). *Forgive and Forget: Healing the hurts we don't deserve.* New York, NY: HarperCollins.

Smedes, Lewis. (1996). *The art of forgiving.* Nashville: Moorings, a division of Random House.

Stanton L. Jones & Mark A. Yarhouse. (2000) *Homosexuality: The Use of Scientific Research in the Church's Moral Debate.* Downers Grove, Ill.: InterVarsity Press.

Yancey, Philip. (1997). *What's so amazing about grace?* Grand Rapids, Zondervan.